SUN DANCE

PHOTOGRAPHY AND TEXT
BY MICHAEL CRUMMETT

FALCON PRESS

HELENA, MONTANA

Design, typesetting, and other prepress work by Falcon Press, Helena, Montana. Printed in the United States.

ISBN 1-56044-201-8

Library of Congress Cataloging-in-Publication Data

Crummett, Michael, 1948-
    Sundance: the fiftieth anniversry Crow Indian Sun Dance / by
    Michael Crummett.
        p.   cm.
    Includes bibliographical references.
    ISBN 1-56044-201-8
    1. Sun dance—Montana—Crow Indian Reservation—History. 2.Crow
Indians—Religion and mythology. 3. Crow Indians—Rites and ceremo-
nies. 4. Crow Indian Reservation (Mont.)—Social life and customs.
I. Title
E99.C92C78 1993
299'.74—dc20   93-1567
                                                      CIP

Front cover photo: The Sun Dance formally began when the dancers assembled at the fire circle and "whistled up" the sun as it broke over the horizon.

Dedicated to all Sun Dancers throughout the country. May the Crow-Shoshone Sun Dance that William Big Day reintroduced in 1941 to the Apsáalooke people in Pryor flourish for another fifty years...and beyond.

C O N T E N T S

In July of 1941 my dad, William Big Day, had a Sun Dance in Pryor, Montana, on the Crow Indian Reservation. It was two years before that date that my dad vowed to bring the Sun Dance back to his people if I lived through my illness.

In 1991, it turned into fifty. Since it was turning to fifty, I like to put up the Sun Dance for my people; and I'm positively sure it needs to be documented for all the people, and also for my four boys who some of these days would like to have a Sun Dance, and can go back and look at the pictures and read the story and continue. Down in the future, I'd like to see this book be used for education throughout the nation and the wide world, not only for the Indian, but as well the white people—the people that stands under the red, white and blue flag.

Because that these cultural things had been lost—I'll mention some of them: the Bear Dance Song, the Pipe Dance and, I think they call it Meat Whistle Song—so now this Sun Dance, I would like to keep it for the future. The Crow Tribe should keep the Sun Dance to pray for the people and the sick, and well as for even the white people. If we have some document, like this book, it won't be lost like other ceremonies.

I asked Mike to take the photographs of this Fiftieth Anniversary Sun Dance because that he was our friend for about twenty-three years. He's like part of the family, and I trusted him that he would do a good job.

I thank Mike and those people that help me, that those that read this book could understand our culture, to exchange cultures, so we can understand each other better.

I started building a bridge to and from the white world. I have laid the framework out for my people's future generations.

Heywood Big Day
Pryor, Montana

P R E F A C E

On a spring morning in 1992, I received a visit from Heywood Big Day and Michael Crummett. They had come to show me slides of photographs that Michael had taken the previous year, at Heywood's request, of the fiftieth anniversary of a Crow Sun Dance ceremony.

As the staff and I watched the slides flow across the screen, it became evident that the images were wonderfully sensitive. Narrative, yes, since their purpose was to record an event. But Michael had taken great care to infuse each frame with an artist's careful attention to aesthetic consider-ations. It became clear, as both men talked, that the purpose of the photographs was to share a deeply religious ceremony with non-Crow people. Heywood's desire to encourage greater public understanding of the Crow religion and its historic ceremonies might be accomplished through exhibiting these images.

Michael Crummett's sensitivity to the various facets of the ceremony reflected Heywood Big Day's careful instructions. Cameras had not been allowed at previous Sun Dance ceremonies and this event had to be carefully and accurately recorded. When Michael completed the first prints, he and Heywood discussed where the exhibition could receive the widest exposure, for both the Crow and non-Crow people. Billings, Mon-tana situated next to the Crow Reservation and with a public art museum, seemed the logical site. The staff and I concurred.

I want to thank Heywood, Michael, and those who were willing to have their roles in the ceremony recorded for this beautiful exhibition of forty-four color and black-and-white photographs. These Sun Dance photographs will be on exhibit at the Yellowstone Art Center in June, July and August, 1993.

Donna M. Forbes, Director
Yellowstone Art Center
Billings, Montana

ACKNOWLEDGMENTS

The Golden Anniversary Crow Sun Dance projects have become reality through the efforts of many individuals and organizations. My gratitude is foremost extended to my dear friend, Heywood Big Day, who, like his bold, precedent-setting father, had a dream .... and accomplished it. With the foresight and conviction of a visionary, Heywood not only decided to host a historic Sun Dance, or Big Lodge Ceremony, but also courageously chose to have it photographed, something rarely done. Many thanks, Heywood, for entrusting me with the opportunity, challenge and responsibilities of documenting your sacred Sun Dance. Your abiding friendship, guidance, encouragement and prayers throughout this entire evolution have inspired me to glorious peaks that I did not know even existed. I appreciate you letting me be your instrument to preserve this holy rite in pictures for Crow Indians, and, hopefully, to create greater cross-cultural understanding of the Sun Dance among all people. Aho!

I am most grateful, also, to the members of the Big Day tribe for your hearty companionship, open-door assistance and delectably tasty frybread. I am moved by the fact that you have made me and my family so much a part of you and yours.

In an effort to secure funding for the cost of producing the exhibition of photographs and of researching and interviewing in the field, many individuals on and off the Crow Reservation wrote letters of support. Among those to whom I am grateful: Heywood Big Day, Crow Sun Dance Chief; John Pretty On Top, Crow Sun Dance Chief; Larson Medicine Horse, Crow Sun Dance Chief; Angela Russell, Montana State Representative; Bill Yellowtail, Montana State Senator; Pat Williams, Montana's United States Representative; and, Nicholas Vrooman, State Folklorist and Director of Folklife Programs with the Montana Arts Council.

I am also thankful for the board and staff of the Yellowstone Art

Center. Their willingness and commitment to sponsor this special project is most commendable. Donna Forbes, Gordon McConnell, Terry Karson, and Marilynn Miller have displayed unflagging determination, faith and enthusiasm in creating a major exhibition of Fiftieth Anniversary Sun Dance photographs.

My appreciation is likewise extended to the Montana Arts Council for its support and grant assistance. Nicholas Vrooman, multi-talented MAC Folklife Director, shared meaningful insights concerning project development and always focused his attention on the forest instead of the trees.

I am indebted to those who shared their personal Big Lodge perspectives during our tape-recorded interviews: Heywood, Mary Lou and Bill Big Day; Philip Beaumont; Clara Rides Horse Smells; Gordon Plain Bull; Mary Elizabeth Rondeaux Berg; Father Randolph Graczyk; and Mick Fedullo. Without their accounts, there would be no story.

Many thanks to several people who helped me separate the wheat from the chaff in the manuscript. Heywood and his son, Derek White, kept me honest and accurate. Father Randolph—a Catholic priest, Sun Dancer, and Crow linguist—scrutinized and enhanced my language usage. Fellow writer Mick Fedullo, with his keen eye and careful copy editing, cut away blubber and extra pounds from an overweight original.

Last but surely not least, I am indebted to Linda, Justin and Nathan for their accomodation during research and development of the manuscript. For months, they accepted the fact that the only time I would be at the dining room table was—not at mealtime as usual—but at two or three in the morning with my tapes, transcripts, texts, spiral notebooks and sharpened pencils. They are glad, as I am, to have the draft go forward and for their dad to come back.

Michael Crummett
Billings, Montana

In 1988 Heywood Big Day, a personal friend for over twenty years, approached me with his vision and plans to hold a Fiftieth Anniversary Crow Sun Dance. It was Heywood's father, William Big Day, who reintroduced this sacred ceremony to the Crow Indians in 1941 after a sixty-six year hiatus. Heywood wanted me to document this historic ceremony through still photographs for the purpose of cultural preservation, educational advancement and greater understanding by non-Indians of this most spiritual Plains Indian religion.

Having intermittently lived with and worked for the Crow Indians through two decades and knowing that photographing a Sun Dance was summarily forbidden, I declined Heywood's invitation. A year later, he came calling once more with the same proposal but was kindly extended another rejection. After several more requests, I agreed to at least consider the possibilities.

In a traditional and holy rite that took place by the waters of Pryor Creek, Heywood painted me with ashes to consecrate our first step together, blazing a new, unfamiliar trail.

On several occasions we conferred in the dark, heated confines of Heywood's sweat lodge in Pryor. We discussed and prayed about the proposition extensively in a concerted effort to explore the project's propriety with due reverence and respect. Heywood convinced me that, on this occasion, photographing his Golden Anniversary Crow Sun Dance was indeed the right thing to do, and that he would guide me along the way with his instructions, assistance and blessings. And so I consented to document this historic ceremony. In a traditional and holy rite that took place by the waters of Pryor Creek, Heywood painted me with ashes to consecrate our first step together, blazing a new, unfamiliar trail.

The Sun Dance was but the culminating event in a long continuum of many events over an eight-month period. Starting on the winter solstice, 1990, there were four Medicine Bundle Ceremonies through the winter. Then, four Outdoor Prayer Services took place throughout the spring and early summer of 1991. Next was a magnificent trip to the top of the Big Horn Mountains to hunt two buffalo for the post-Sun Dance feast. Other journeys were made to the Pryor Mountains to harvest lodgepole pine, aspen and fir trees for lodge construction. The actual Sun Dance was merely the last in a long line of ceremonial activities.

Through word of mouth, press coverage and an authorized program handed out at the Sun Dance, Big Day made everyone, both participants and spectators, aware of the fact that I would be photographing the ceremonial and was the only one permitted to do so. I was not to photograph: 1) with a flash or strobe; 2) from anywhere inside the lodge; 3) certain segments that were considered too sacred for public consumption; and 4) those dancers who expressed their wishes beforehand not to be photographed. Without exception, I rigidly adhered to Heywood's parameters, as well as my own.

After the Sun Dance was completed and the film processed, Heywood, Mary Lou and I reviewed hundreds of images. The Big Days were very much pleased with what they saw. Not one photo had to be yanked because of questionable content. Moreover, they gave their hearty support, unanimous approval and ultimate consent to make another step with the visuals. But where would that next footprint lead? We knew something was there, but what was it, and how far should we take it? We had not discussed future directions.

Heywood's closing statement in the official Sun Dance brochure left little doubt as to what orientation he would assume with these historically significant photographs. "Our Crow belief in the religious importance of the Sun Dance," Big Day affirmed, "is something we are proud of and wish to share with people of all backgrounds." Like his father, William Big Day, and in the spirit of his dad's brother-in-law, Chief Plenty Coups (who urged the Crows to be educated and to acculturate, rather than assimilate, with whites), Heywood wanted to bridge gaps and facilitate mutual under-standing. We had to go further than just making the photographs.

To reach out in the truest and most wide-ranging sense, we approached the Yellowstone Art Center in Billings with a proposal for an exhibition of the Golden Anniversary Crow Sun Dance images. This nationally re-nowned arts museum benefits a local, state, regional, country-wide and international audience. More than any other institution within 600 miles, it would be the ideal place to achieve a respectful, hallowed, non-political treatment of the subject. The staff and board enthusiastically endorsed the idea, agreed to sponsor the project and scheduled an exhibition for the summer of 1993.

Obviously, the entire story could not be told in pictures. Too many vignettes in the whole progression would be overlooked if a narrative was excluded. Too many of Big Day's captivating tales and enchanting meta-phors would be lost if his words were not embraced. There was a definite story to be told: Heywood wanted to tell it; Falcon Press wanted to publish it; and I was Big Day's writing instrument to get it done.

It goes without saying that not all tribes, not all medicine men, not all Sun Dance chiefs would choose this path of exposure. After all, Sun Dances represent the most sacred religious experience of Great Plains Indians. For the non-Indian populace, they have remained shrouded in mystery because of where they are held, the lack of publicity and the fact that they are not photographed. Nicholas Vrooman, State Folklorist with the Montana Arts Council, commented on Heywood's bold spirit, "It's a courageous act that Heywood has taken to bring the Sun Dance out for the benefit of all people. It's very courageous because there's a lot of risk involved but also an equal degree of good to come out of it!"

The journey to publicize Big Day's Sun Dance has actually been evolutionary in nature. The notion to create an exhibition and/or publish a book did not strike us until months after the Golden Sun Dance concluded. It was neither an accident nor an original resolution but, as time went by, somewhere in between. Once we had committed ourselves to these goals and had indeed made strides down those pathways, Heywood held a Medicine Bundle Ceremony at the First United Methodist Church in Billings. To maintain an ethical path, the Big Days felt that the bundles should be opened. On that occasion, the first of its kind off the reservation, supplications were uttered on prayer smoke to the One Divine Being, asking his blessings on the projects so that they could be kept as sacred as the subject matter itself.

We do not purport that this narrative is an academic treatise on Sun Dances. Several other fine books and journal articles exist which assume that function and it is not our intention to duplicate those efforts. This is the story of one Sun Dance, a very special, historical Crow Indian Sun Dance, sponsored and conducted by Heywood Big Day, who, as a dying infant a half-century before, was the inspiration for his father to reintroduce the Sun Dance to the Crows after a sixty-six-year void. Thanks to William, Heywood, Tom Yellowtail, John Pretty On Top, Larson Medicine Horse, John Cummins and many other medicine men and Sun Dance chiefs, the Big Lodge is alive, well, and thriving among the *Apsáalooke*.

Michael Crummett
Billings, Montana

SUN DANCE

The little Crow Indian baby lay dying. At ten months of age, he had hardly grown and was as small as the day in June, 1938, when he was born. He had ceased eating and drinking, and the outlook was grim.

His parents, William Big Day and Annie Lion Shows Big Day, were at a loss. They had adopted the baby from Cecelia Lion Shows on Father's Day, 1938, to give him a fresh, healthy start. In the traditional Crow way, a sick or troubled child is adopted by another family in order to provide a new beginning. From Pryor, Montana, they took their child to Billings, some thirty miles away, where they hoped the white doctors would remedy his illness. Instead, the physicians diagnosed their son with double pneumonia and informed the parents that he did not have long to live.

With tears and disbelief, the couple returned with the boy to their log cabin. Patches of dirty, crusty snow still dotted the landscape around this Crow village when the local Catholic priest was summoned to administer last rites. In desperation, William undressed his failing son and took his limp, naked body out into the sharp mountain air. Greeting a new day and a rising sun, Big Day held the child heavenward and asked *Akbaatatdia*, the One Divine Being, to spare his only child. "If you will let my boy live," he prayed, "I promise I will bring the Sun Dance back to my people."

Within four hours, the infant began to drink water. Soon he was eating beef soup, a thin, nutritious broth. Miraculously, William's son made a full recovery and regained his health completely.

Faced with such a traumatic experience, William Big Day's vow to (sun) dance again was a natural response for a spiritual Plains Indian. In the 1800s the Sun Dance was a culturally paramount, supremely sacred ceremony of religious purification and renewal. Over the course of four days and three nights, Sun Dancers prayed to the Great Spirit, abstained from food and water, fluttered under the sizzling summer sun, suffered

In the 1800s the Sun Dance was a culturally paramount, supremely sacred ceremony of religious purification and renewal.

physical torment from self-inflicted "piercing," and trilled through eagle bone whistles in an effort to transcend the actual confines of the Sun Dance lodge and reach a most-personal spiritual realm. Self-denial, bodily pain and an endless stream of tobacco-smoke prayers to the Almighty were offered as a testimonial of the individual's genuine purpose of attaining good health, locating buffalo, gaining greater power over an enemy, stealing horses or manifesting revenge.

Big Day witnessed his first Sun Dance in 1938, and actually participated during the summers of 1939 and 1940 at Fort Washakie, Wyoming. Under the revered Shoshone medicine man, John Trehero, whose Indian name was Rainbow, William had several moving experiences. For one, he discovered a large lump coming through his lower ribs and became very ill on the second day of the ceremony. He could not move and could not dance because it hurt so badly. Rainbow finally got him up to the Sun Dance Center Pole and began doctoring William with his medicine feathers. By the time the treatment was complete, the lump had vanished and Big Day was able to dance back to his station, then finish the grueling ceremony. Both men had a vision and acknowledged that, had it not been for that Shoshone Sun Dance healing, William would have died by spring. "I found out," William affirmed, "that this Sun Dance was a great and powerful thing."

Big Day had other prophetic visions in those Shoshone Sun Dances. One occurred at a sunrise ceremony when he saw two Indian men, a Shoshone and a Crow, greeting each other with right arms extended. The red profiles that William saw on the horizon created a circle of exchange and foretold the coming of the Shoshone Sun Dance to the Crow Indians.

Furthermore, Big Day saw Rainbow's medicine feathers being given to him. William was a visionary who long had a genuine calling to help his people. He was sincere in his desire to cure illness and to incite the Crows to goodness and religiosity. To reach these goals, he had even tried Catholicism, and then peyote in the Native American Church, but both practices left him incomplete. When he envisioned himself with the Shoshone medicine man's feathers, Big Day finally realized that his Sun Dance (and the year-round belief system that it implied) would afford the Crows the ultimate Indian Way of spirituality.

In the summer of 1941 William Big Day kept his promise to *Akbaatatdía* and conducted the first Crow Sun Dance since 1875. For sixty-six years, the Crows had abstained from this sacred ceremony for reasons ranging from the federal government's policy of assimilating all Indian people, to white reservation missionaries denouncing the indigenous religious practices as evil and pagan to internal tribal reassessment of the ceremony. But since the life of his baby boy had been spared (which coincided with these other influences in his spiritual development), Big Day's vow would be fulfilled and his place in Crow Indian history indelibly imprinted.

Philip Beaumont, a respected Crow elder and camp crier who has served as a tribal spokesman before Congress, tribunals and the public, was twenty years old when that first Shoshone-Crow Sun Dance took place. Of his paternal clan uncle, Philip recalled, "I thought that William was very bold. He was a man of strong character. He realized that this [Sun Dance] had to happen. He was brave in a sense he knew there might be some repercussions, I mean, if the government ever stepped in. There were two purposes: one, he had a son who was going down, down, down of ill health. He had that to consider. Secondly, he had to consider all of the young men that had to go to war. He wanted safe return for every one of those individuals. He took the initiative and went ahead.

"So when he came to the point of establishing the Sun Dance," Beaumont continued, "I think everybody already knew his qualities as a leader. We were all anxious. We wanted to see what was going to happen. You

In the summer of 1941 William Big Day kept his promise to Akbaatatdía *and conducted the first Crow Sun Dance since 1875.*

could see the enthusiasm of the people. Everyone came. The encampment was big, I mean, it was a big circle of tepees [around the Sun Dance lodge]. So, even outsiders, outside of the Sun Dancers, a lot of people, fasted along with the Sun Dancers. The time was right and ripe!"

The Crows' first Sun Dance in Pryor, in 1941, was actually William's fourth. Shoshone Medicine Man Rainbow had been invited to help Big Day with all of the ensuing responsibilities. Participating were twenty-three dancers, one of whom was Anglo but married to a Shoshone woman. On the first day, William's vision about the passing of the medicine feathers became a reality. According to Big Day, "John Trehero got up and gave the feathers to me, and said, 'I give these feathers to you. You can help your people when they are sick. You can doctor them in the Sun Dance, and in everything that they might need help—help them with these feathers. The power of the Sun Dance is through them feathers.' Then I was standing towards the sun and raised my hands to the sun, and thanked Him for finding a way [for me] to help my people." After that first Sun Dance, Big Day was convinced that "Some kind of life came back to the Indian again!" (Voget Interview with William Big Day, 1946, Page 9).

In 1942, William Big Day participated in the second Shoshone-Crow Sun Dance in Pryor, sponsored by Frank Hawk and conducted by Tom Compton, another Shoshone Medicine Man. In addition to sickness, the abiding concerns of this ceremony, held against the backdrop of World War II, were the prayers for peace and for the safe return of Crow soldiers fighting for the United States on foreign soil. From 1941 to 1946, there were nineteen Sun Dances, half of which took place outside of Crow Agency, tribal headquarters of the *Apsáalooke* or "Children of the large-beaked bird." During this period the Sun Dance was firmly re-established among the Crow Indians; it has been conducted regularly ever since.

In the summer of 1991 a very special Sun Dance was held in Pryor, at

WILLIAM BIG DAY, SECOND FROM LEFT, WITH UNIDENTIFIED CROW INDIAN SUN DANCERS
IN PRYOR, MONTANA, DURING THE HISTORIC 1941 SUN DANCE. WILLIAM VOWED TO
REESTABLISH THE SUN DANCE AMONG THE CROW PEOPLE IF AKBAATATDÍA, THE ONE
DIVINE BEING, SPARED THE LIFE OF HIS SON, HEYWOOD. (PHOTO BY K.F.R.)

the exact spot where the first one was conducted fifty years before. The historical significance of this ceremonial was that it marked the Golden Anniversary. It was exceptional because Heywood Big Day, the medicine man who sponsored and conducted the 1991 ceremony and dedicated it to his father, was the same person who, as a baby boy near death fifty-two years before, was the inspiration for William Big Day's reintroducing the Shoshone Sun Dance to the Crow in 1941. Heywood was a living testimonial to the strength of the Sun Dance tradition, truly an unbroken circle of love, spiritual rejuvenation and cultural rededication.

Heywood never went into a Sun Dance while his father was living. He often approached his dad about participating in the sacred ceremony but William always responded, "You don't have any reason to be goin' in. You don't just go in and see what it's all about. There's got to be a good reason and you don't have one. One of these days, you'll know when, you'll know what to do. Once I go over the hill, you know where everything is and you know how to handle it!"

Glimpses of another memorable conversation that took place back in 1967 came rushing to the surface. "My dad," Heywood began, "just before he passed away, on his last breath, he was telling me that some of these days, I know very well, you gonna have to have a Sun Dance. And so try and get it the right way. He said he hoped this Sun Dance could go all the way up to 100 years so my grandchildren could have a ceremonial like these white man centennials. After so many years, after he passed away, I thought about it.

"So I went into my first Sun Dance around the age of thirty," Heywood continued, "right after my dad passed away. See, I was raised with this medicine bundle and I knew how to handle it and everything. But I was afraid to use it. The reason I was afraid is there's some stiff laws when you use this medicine. [A Sun Dance Chief must lead a virtuous life.] If I break one of these laws, what's going to happen to me or my family?"

Around 1968, Heywood went into two Sun Dances. Other years he would go in three times. He concentrated on prayer and practiced the spiritual power. He worked with his uncle, John Cummins, during several ceremonies. He was even tutored by Rainbow, who officially transferred the sacred attributes of William's feathers to son Heywood. Within four or five years, Heywood felt that he was confident enough to use the medicine bundle, and the power that came with it.

The seeds having been sown, dreams of a Golden Anniversary Sun Dance came to Heywood in 1985. He gathered his wife, Mary Lou, and four sons—Derek, Junior (Heywood, Jr.), William and Jace—around the dining room table for a family meeting. Proposing the idea was simple compared to realizing the responsibilities of such an undertaking. Much work and expense would be incurred. Personal sacrifice would be required. After the exploratory discussions, the Big Days stood as one in their support of a Fiftieth Anniversary Crow Sun Dance, an historic tribute to father/grandfather, William.

It was good they had years to pursue their vision. With such a major project, Heywood would obviously need more assistance than his family could provide. For one, he wanted spiritual guidance. In October, 1990, he invited his Big Lodge clan uncle, Alex Medicine Horse, to his home for a bath, counsel and prayers in the sweat lodge. Medicine Horse was impressed with the notion and gave Heywood his blessing.

The next month, Heywood called together six important Crow spiritual leaders for a council in Pryor. Assembled from every corner of the reservation were Thomas Yellowtail, preeminent Crow medicine man and Sun Dance Chief (though retired); John Pretty On Top, Yellowtail's hand-picked and sole authorized successor; Larson Medicine Horse, Shoshone-Crow Sun Dance Chief and Big Horn County Sheriff, as well as his father, Thomas Medicine Horse; Tom Big Lake, Crow Sun Dance medicine man; and Alex Medicine Horse, Big Lodge clan uncle. The seven entered Big Day's sweat lodge for four searing rounds.

"Here's what I'd like to do," declared Heywood. "I want to put up a Sun Dance for this coming summer. My dad brought this Sun Dance back fifty years ago this comin' '91. That feather and I, we grew up together. I will need your advice, help and blessing. This is gonna be my first time that I'm gonna run it. And I'd like to have all you people, especially the Big Lodge. I like to have your help so I'll be on the right track. I grew up with this medicine, but yet, when there's lots of commotion, when there's gonna be a real heavy power spirit, here's where I need your guidance. If there is any high-powered spirit, I may get off the line or something. So if I'm off the line, I wanna have somebody to fall back on. So, I'm calling on you gentlemen to help me. I want you to be a kind of a board of directors, or you can call it my guidance. If I have some questions, I would need some advice from you people."

Those present agreed to help with their time, energy and prayers. From Pryor, word hit the moccasin telegraph that Heywood Big Day would be sponsoring as well as conducting the Fiftieth Anniversary Crow Indian Sun Dance. The news spread like wildfire across the reservation, throughout Indian Country and beyond.

In December of 1990, Big Day held the first of four Medicine Bundle Ceremonies to officially, publicly and prayerfully usher in his Sun Dance. "My dad was telling me," Heywood explained, "that when you're sponsoring a Sun Dance, you have to open the medicine bundle four times and you have to use the sun. When the sun goes up to the south all the way up to the end, and turns back to the north again [winter solstice], during at that time, no more than four days before or four days after, you have to have that medicine bundle opened."

From Pryor, word hit the moccasin telegraph that Heywood Big Day would be sponsoring as well as conducting the Fiftieth Anniversary Crow Indian Sun Dance.

The other Sun Dance chiefs were invited to Pryor for that first Opening and Prayer Ceremony but could not make it. The roads were icy on that Friday night, four days before Christmas, and the temperature was a bone-chilling thirty degrees below zero. Heywood held the service with the assistance of his "altar boy," Samuel Plain Feather.

A Crow's medicine, or *xapaalia*, comes from *Akbaatatdía* through the natural world and empowers the holder with mystical abilities and spiritual strengths. The objects, symbolic of his Medicine Fathers, may have come through a dream, from a family member or friend who hands the medicine down, or as a result of a vision quest experience. Tom Yellowtail explains, "The real power comes from God, the Maker of All Things Above, but it is passed on to us through our Medicine Fathers. All of the Medicine Fathers live in Nature. So the Indians are able to receive direct blessings and gifts from beyond this world we see, from God, through our Medicine Fathers. Powers and knowledge are never given to anyone who does not live according to the rules that must be observed" (Yellowtail, 15-16).

Heywood received his personal medicine, or *iaxpaalia*, from his father. William Big Day acquired his gifts from Rainbow, who obtained his medicine from Seven Arrows, Chief of the Little People. Among his special pieces are bald and golden eagle feathers, black speckled feathers, otter fur and mountain lion fur. The medicine is always stored in a medicine bundle, which is kept in a safe place until it is brought out for a specific purpose.

Heywood's four Medicine Bundle Ceremonies were held in Pryor, Montana. The first one took place at St. Charles Mission, the others at Pryor Elementary School. A rug was initially placed on the cold linoleum floor. Then a buffalo hide was laid on top of that. Completing the altar, a Pendleton blanket was added and finally Big Day's medicine bundle. In front of the blankets, a four-foot-long wooden dowel had been planted in a quart Mason jar full of dirt. Tethered to the top of the dowel was an eagle plume and a pair of raptor's talons in a "C" shaped representation of a bison's horns. This was symbolic of the Sun Dance Center Pole from which a stuffed bald eagle and mounted buffalo head are suspended. Nearby, a Griswold frying pan full of glowing coals was positioned on two bricks.

With the medicine men seated on the floor, facing east, unobstructed, cedar man Samuel Plain Feather sprinkled the cedar sprigs onto the hot embers. Clouds of aromatic smoke rose from the sweet Indian incense. Heywood began to pray in his native Crow tongue as Samuel "smudged" the medicine bundle, holding and moving it through the purifying smoke. The prayers ascended heavenwards and in all directions on the trails of the burning cedar.

Philip Beaumont, camp crier and oft-appointed Crow/English interpretor for Big Day's Medicine Bundle Ceremonies, detailed sweet cedar's importance. "First, we regard cedar as a gift from Mother Earth. Second, when you start using the cedar, as the smoke and aroma fill the air, it is understood that burning of cedar is a kind of spiritual cleansing and allows the Great Spirit to come into your realm. So we are very careful about using cedar."

The medicine bundles were soon opened and their contents displayed after each medicine object was individually smudged. Heywood then smoked some sacred tobacco, in the form of cigarettes, to provide the medium through which his supplications for a successful Sun Dance would rise from the firmament and fall on the ears of the One Divine Being.

Tobacco has been sanctified ever since Chief No Vitals received it during a vision quest in the 1660s. "No Vitals not only led the people to their promised land [Montana and Wyoming] but at Devil's Lake in North Dakota he fasted and received a gift of sacred tobacco seeds. In Crow legend, No Vitals was not always the recipient of the gift, but there was agreement that the character and the destiny of the Crow people were linked to the sacred tobacco. In the Crow view, gift of the sacred tobacco assured the overcoming of their enemies, and hence they were destined to be a great and powerful people" (Voget, 5). Throughout all aspects of the Sun Dance preparations, practices and progression, tobacco played an abiding, integral part.

Guests at the Medicine Bundle Ceremonies were invited to form a prayer line. Pledged Sun Dancers, supporters, family and friends introduced themselves one at a time and whispered a specific prayer request to one of the medicine men. They next gave holy tobacco to the spiritual leader as an offering to the Almighty. When all had shared the secret desires of their hearts, the medicine men lit the first of many cigarettes and began to pray aloud in Crow: one tobacco, one prayer, for one individual. Spiritual wishes rose on the cigarette smoke to the heavens and to the First Maker. When that particular supplication was completed, the medicine man would extinguish that tobacco, light another and proceed to the next prayer. For hours, scores of holy cigarettes were smoked by the Crow medicine men, each representing a personal petition.

HEYWOOD BIG DAY LIGHTS A HOLY PRAYER SMOKE AT ONE OF THE OUTDOOR CEREMONIES.

Combined with the smells of cedar and tobacco smoke were the mixed sounds of voice, drum and whistle. Gordon Plain Bull, Heywood's brother-in-law, brought his drum and recruited a half-dozen men to help with the beat and song. Junior, Billy and Jace Big Day were among those who chimed in. Encircling a drum whose size was the equivalent of two truck tires stacked together, the six played and sang special Sun Dance songs. The penetrating pulse of the drum and monotonic melody of the vocables of the men were accented with the sharp, high-pitched choruses of several women. Interspersed between these sounds and the smoke were the occasional whistlings by the spiritual leaders on eagle bone pipes clenched between their teeth.

After all phases of the ritual had been performed and the medicine was once again smudged and returned to the bundle, the holy ceremony culminated with a traditional Crow feed. Mary Lou Big Day, Heywood's wife and head cook at Pryor Elementary, coordinated the food preparations. Mary Lou said, "I knew what I was gonna be cookin'—the soup [vegetable beef], frybread, cake, coffee and Indian pudding [Juneberry or blueberry]. I had to get all of that ready. I did figure for quite a few but I never do measure things 'cause I go by my mind."

The Medicine Bundle Ceremony was held in December, 1990, and again in January, February and March of 1991. Each ceremony took place within four days, either way, of the full moon of each month. Big Day and Plain Feather had the assistance of medicine men John Pretty on Top, Larson Medicine Horse and their "altar boys" at the last three prayer services.

After "Old Man Winter" and his snow retreated from Pryor and spring arrived, officially marked by the first claps of thunder, Big Day knew that it was time to hold the first of four outdoor preparatory sessions. That rite took place at the actual site planned for the Sun Dance. It was not coincidence, but rather a welling of power that this occurred at the exact location of that first Crow Sun Dance fifty years before.

Regarding the Outdoor Ceremony, Heywood detailed the schedule and contents. "When it's a full moon in April, that's the time we started practicing the Sun Dance. We put a little shade, like a curtain, and we built a fire and we dressed as Sun Dancers. We have to have a whistle [the long, hollow bone of an eagle's wing]. We have to have a [eagle] plume, just like the regular Sun Dance. We have to practice on that when it's a full moon, April, May, June and July. You could even call them 'dress rehearsals.'

"It's a prayer Sun Dance," he continued. "We're praying so the people could be healed during the time of the Sun Dance and have a good relationship with all the Indians. I don't care what kind of a tribe they

Let it be said that every medicine man or Sun Dance Chief has the flexibility and liberty to put his own stamp on an activity.

were, the doors were open. I prayed for a good spirit and have a calm night. We ask the Spirit so they could have a safe journey comin' over and participate on this Sun Dance and a safe journey goin' back home. And also for the Crow Nation. And also my prayers were goin' through all four directions. All them little details, we have to pray about it. That's why we would like to pray about it and talk about it. This Sun Dance, it takes a lot of time and preparations."

Like the Medicine Bundle Ceremonies, the Outdoor Prayer Services took place within four days of the full moon. Time-marking full moons not only held a central place in this culture so integrated with natural elements but also provided a practical quality—light. In the olden days, Indians obviously did not have lanterns or flashlights. Their sources of illumination were the sun, moon and fire. An evening Outdoor Ceremony held at optimum moonlight alongside a blazing bonfire would utilize two of their three original sources—and one of those was contingent on the third! So when the last speck of sun dipped beneath the western horizon and the face of the moon peered down on Pryor through the afterglow of twilight, the services began.

Let it be said that every medicine man or Sun Dance Chief has the flexibility and liberty to put his own stamp on an activity. Indeed, there are certain formats and procedures that must take place along the Sun Dance continuum, but it is up to the individual practitioner to interpret the ceremony, rather than translate it verbatim.

Before the Outdoor Ceremony started, four specific sites were established and aligned. The point of origination was on the eastern horizon where the sun would introduce a new day. Born, raised and having lived in Pryor for his entire half-century life, Big Day knew, even in the dark, where that spot was at any given time of the year. The second position was where the Center Pole would be; that was a given because it would be

HEYWOOD BIG DAY STANDS
AGAINST HIS "NEST" AT THE
OUTDOOR CEREMONY.

erected exactly where it had stood during the 1941 Sun Dance. Proceeding westward, the third placement was the firepit which had to extend the imaginary line that the previous two points created. The fourth, final and westernmost station was a canvas curtain hung from three upright poles. This served as a symbolic "slice" of the Sun Dance lodge itself.

In explaining the partition, Heywood said, "Even the birds, they do have a nest. Even the mice have a nest. Even the ant has a nest. Every kind of a nature here in this earth has got a nest. If I don't have any canvas curtain, I won't have any nest. That represents the nest, the Big Lodge. There's where our life is. That's where we're livin'. That's our home. Standing in the west, lookin' toward the east, everything's all lined up. The sunrise, Center Pole, fire and curtain—all four are in a straight line."

The man in charge of the fire at the Outdoor Ceremonies had to be a contemporary warrior who had gained honor and repute in the armed services. Fred Turnsback was chosen. He had a successful stretch in the military, having enlisted and re-enlisted a total of four times. Under pastel skies, Turnsback kindled the firewood that stood in a tepee arrangement.

Once the flames were flickering to the rhythm of the Sun Dance songs rising from drum and voice, Heywood sprinkled holy cedar. He prayed as the sacred smoke cleansed the hearts and minds of those present. In addition to his own prayers at the Outdoor Ceremony, Big Day called on Big Lodge clan uncles and other esteemed veterans to invoke the First Maker's blessings on the Golden Anniversary Sun Dance. Alex Medicine Horse, John Pretty On Top and Samuel Plain Feather were respected individuals who fulfilled those supplications. Carson Walks Over Ice was called to the fireside, offered tobacco, and asked to tell of a war deed in which *Akbaatatdía's* protection and blessing were spiritually present.

Heywood translated Carson's story from Crow to English. Carson was a paratrooper in Vietnam at the height of the war. On this occasion, he was dropped behind enemy lines. After free-falling for what seemed an eternity, he pulled his rip cord but his parachute did not open. The ground was getting closer, he was descending faster, and time was running out. He tried activating his secondary chute but to no avail. The voice of the Great Spirit came to Walks Over Ice and said, "Don't worry, it'll open." Seconds later, at the last possible moment, the emergency chute blossomed. Words from *Akbaatatdía* continued, "Once you go down to the bottom, be prepared!" After he landed, machine gun bullets started flying at him from all directions. Somehow, he managed to evade the enemy's firepower and made a successful escape, but not before he was forced to kill numerous Vietcong in self-defense. Unscathed, he returned to his forces, and to more heroic war deeds in the coming months.

Carson told Heywood, "I came back [to Crow Country]. For my [good] luck, it is yours, my son." He prayed that the same Great Spirit that was with him in foreign battle would bestow abundant blessings on Big Day and on the Sun Dancers who would be waging spiritual battles during the Golden Anniversary Ceremony. He desired that every participant, and the Crow Tribe, would enjoy the same success that he had experienced, and that the prayers of all the people would be answered. In adherence to Crow custom, Walks Over Ice was then presented with several gifts for his story and invocation.

All four of these Outdoor Ceremonies were nearly identical in form and format. As the sponsor-pledger of the Sun Dance, Heywood was dressed in his radiant red skirt, whistle and plume. The singers, seated to the south, beat the drum to the first of four Sun Dance songs. Big Day blew his eagle wing bone whistle and danced from his "nest" to the fire and back again. At the third Ceremony, his Big Lodge clan uncle, Crow medicine man and Sun Dance Chief John Pretty On Top, came to Pryor to pray and dance with him.

The final Outdoor Ceremony took place the night before the Sun Dance started. The only difference between the four services was that the fireplace was moved easterly toward the Center Pole position by four paces each time. The ashes of the last rehearsal fire ended up being, in twenty-four hours, right outside the Sun Dance lodge's west wall, just behind Heywood.

The months between October, 1990 and June, 1991 were busy with planning, preparations and ceremonies. That July, 1991 was downright hectic. The start of the Sun Dance, set for Thursday evening, July 25, was fast approaching and there was little time not to be working on some specific chore. A hunting trip to the top of the Big Horn Mountains was one such task.

According to *Apsáalooke* tradition, a substantial feast is to be held on the last day of the Sun Dance, after the participants have exited the lodge. Acting on a request from Big Day, Crow administrators approved donating two bison from the tribal herd to feed an expected crowd of 600 - 800 people. The ultimate trick and, as it turned out, time-consuming feat, was to get to the buffalo pasture six hours away from Pryor, make the kills, butcher the carcasses and return home before the meat spoiled in the 100-degree temperatures of July.

When he decided that "today was the day," Heywood quickly assembled the hunting party. Mary Lou accompanied him in the lead, four-wheel-drive Blackfeet Bronco. Son Bill, daughter-in-law Martha, grandkids Elisha, Randolph and nephew Archie Jefferson were in the middle of the caravan. Clan nephew Dennis Beaumont and son Jace brought up the rear in another pickup. It was fortunate that the flat tire on Beaumont's outfit came before they had reached Fort Smith, where they had it repaired. Beyond this small village, fixing a flat would have been downright dangerous on the mountainous ascent.

The choppy drive to the top was a beautiful yet arduous one. It was not just a dirt trail but a veritable rocky route. The vehicles jerked and lunged up steps and over shelves of burnt orange chugwater sandstone. Thick tracts of mountain juniper yielded to spacious clearings of visibility that in turn gave way to sporadic upheavals of plump, rocky outcrops. Occasionally the group would see their destination on the other side of the canyon above Big Horn Lake, a seemingly short distance by sight, but a long, body-jarring drive around the horseshoe-shaped course.

Black Canyon, Windy Point, Lookout and Red Springs—all Big Horn Mountain landmarks—were behind them as sunset lay ahead. Across a gently rolling meadow, which could have passed for an ocean of multi-hued wildflowers, waited the tribal game warden, Jason Shane. His office was the Crow buffalo pasture on top of these sacred Big Horn Mountains; his responsibility was 750 head of brucellosis-free bison. From where they stood, the distinct lights of Hardin, Billings, Laurel, Red Lodge and Lovell, as well as the city glow of Columbus, Cody and Sheridan could be seen in this 360-degree panorama. The perspective was heavenly...down and distant. Not so long ago, all of this land, as far as the eye could touch, had been Crow Country! Jason informed the Big Day party that they would not hunt in the dark but would wait until dawn.

As the day's first light bled over the curves of the earth to their makeshift encampment, the hunters started to stir. Under a thick layer of chalky gray ashes, Heywood rescued and revived a few stubborn embers and soon had a new blaze crackling. A pot of cowboy coffee, hastily boiled, acted like a powerful magnet, pulling everyone out of their toasty bedrolls. The conversation, in Crow, turned to the hunt. With hands and arms flailing in emphasis of his ancient tongue, Big Day told of stories passed on to him about buffalo pursuits in the olden days. Eyes opened, jaws parted and breaths quickened. The tales were more stimulating than the caffeine, in spite of the fact that it was still only 4:15 in the morning.

When Heywood threw his cup's coffee grounds onto the fire and the subsequent cloud of steam mushroomed skyward, it was like a smoke signal that went out to the hunters, butchers and spectators: "Let's go!" People prepared their rifles and knives and piled into their outfits as they would have made ready with horses in the not-so-distant past. With Shane at point, it did not take long before this Sun Dance family came to a small group of the larger herd.

The pickups stopped at a distance as the occupants observed the majestic beasts. Heywood got out of his vehicle and slowly ambled off by himself through the wild daisies, lupine and Indian paintbrush to a point twenty-five yards away. Facing east toward the sun that had just popped its forehead over the faraway prairie horizon, Big Day prayed to the One Divine Being. "I call on You now," he said in Crow, "to be with us on this special day. I ask You to give us a good day and a safe, successful hunt. Bless the buffalo that will be giving up their lives for Your Sun Dance and our feast. The meat will feed many and give us healing power. The spirits will be with us in the Sun Dance and will give us strength. Aho!"

The first herd of bison they encountered numbered roughly two dozen and stood about 150 yards away. The game warden leaned against the side of his truck and braced his 30-30 rifle against the opened door. After drawing a bead on the selected cow, he pulled the trigger. A shot rang out but not a single animal dropped. The herd bolted to the west, with the warden driving his pickup in hot pursuit. The buffalo stampeded over sweet sage, crossed a steep coulee, and high-tailed it up a hill on the other side. Four-wheel truck and two-legged warden were suddenly stymied and could do nothing but watch the frightened animals swiftly ascend to the top in a single file procession.

Big Day prayed to the One Divine Being. "I call on You now," he said in Crow, "to be with us on this special day. I ask You to give us a good day and a safe, successful hunt. Bless the buffalo that will be giving up their lives for Your Sun Dance and our feast."

But it was obvious where they were headed. Silhouetted on the distant ridge against an early morning sea-blue sky stood the lone, old bull of the herd, probably forced into solitary retirement by the younger studs. It was ironic that when a crisis threatened these hump-backed brutes, they were again willing to claim their ostracized elder, seeking safety and sanctuary alongside him.

The Crow buffalo boss returned, stowed his rifle in a gun rack, and the caravan continued. In accordance with traditional Crow mores, which dictate that only one shot by one hunter be permitted to take down a single buffalo, the next try was given to Heywood's son, William. Bill, whose namesake was his famous grandfather, had prepped his gun and spotted in his scope prior to the outing. The caravan then resumed its forward motion in search of more bison. Before too long, the hunters spotted a herd of 200 grazing on nutritious Big Horn grasses in the early morning light. After they were within shooting range, the outfits came to a halt. Jason pointed out several cows that could be targeted while Bill readied himself in the back of the pickup. After wrapping the rifle's leather strap around his left arm, steadying the gun and in a crouched position, William squinted for a few moments and then squeezed the hairpin trigger. A sharp metallic pop exploded and a buffalo dropped. With hardly a pause, a second percussive bullet whizzed out of the barrel and a second bison went down. Two shots, and the quota was suddenly filled.

Of his amazing marksmanship, Bill explained, "I was being prepared. I wanted to have, wanted to feel that right moment with my gun. I worked on my gun all week to make sure it would be very accurate. So the gun did his part and the best part was me aiming right and shooting right. I never experienced anything like that before in my life. Those were my two best experiences of doing something I had never done before."

The Big Day family made its way to the first downed bison. Curious to learn what had happened to their fallen sisters, the remainder of the herd slowly moved closer and closer until they were only twenty paces away.

The game warden drew his razor-sharp bowie knife and slit the chosen one's jugular vein. The procedure was more a formality since the shot from Billy's rifle had killed the animal instantly. The contrast between the size of the buffalo and bullet was potent evidence to the strength of vision of that sharpshooter who had spirituality in his scope.

Heywood moved in to begin carving this special beast, assisted by the others. With Bill and Archie holding the hind legs, and Jace and Dennis stretching the front, Big Day started slicing at the appropriate junctures. His expertise and confidence proved that he had learned well all that was taught him by his parents. Heywood swiftly dismembered the sacred staple of the Plains Indian with the precision of a surgeon coupled with the creativity of a gifted sculptor. In no time, the animal had been quartered and portioned into manageable, indistinguishable chunks of high-protein, low-fat, low-cholesterol, extremely nutritious meat, which covered a twelve-foot-square blue plastic tarp.

True to customary practices, the various innards of the bison were also extracted. Mary Lou cut out the enormous stomach, which was then turned inside out and cleaned. *Apsáalooke* call this honeycombed organ the "Bible" and make tripe soup out of it. The intestines were removed and separated from themselves so that they now were a continuous fifty-foot length of tubing. These were then given to Martha and Elisha who worked their way down the canals, squeezing the excrement out as they went. Later, the intestines would be thoroughly washed in a mountain spring. Back at the kitchen, they would be stuffed with ground or scrap meat and become "Indian sausage." The heart and liver were saved. Even the char-coal-colored tongue, long prized for its taste, symbolic sacredness and status, was cut out of the massive head, a gift for a respected elder or clan

WITH THE SKILL OF A
SURGEON, HEYWOOD BIG DAY
BUTCHERS A BUFFALO COW
FROM THE TRIBAL HERD
DONATED TO THE POST-SUN
DANCE FEAST.

uncle. The head would be stuffed, the hide tanned. Every part of the animal would be used, nothing wasted, just like in days gone by.

After both buffalo were dressed out, Heywood grabbed several pieces of the meat and went off by himself. He laid the chunks down on the ground, faced the east, took off his baseball cap and again began praying in Crow. When he returned to the group, he explained, "I picked up some few pieces to the nature and I took it out a few feet away from where we were butchering. I have to donate to the Mother Nature, to the animals, to the ones eating the meat like the bear and the coyotes and the magpies and all the way up to the eagle. I was asking them to help me on this Sun Dance. Anything that you do, you have to ask and pray and you have to give. Once you received it, you have to give out something. So I shared what we had with [Nature] who had given."

This gesture exemplifies the Crow Indian's attitude towards and harmonious relationship with his natural world. Nature is not seen as something to be mastered or exploited. The *Apsáalooke* believe, as other native peoples do, that by observing nature, man can gain insights into his own life and into his environment. This theme is central to the Sun Dance as well.

After the quarters and parcels were loaded into the pickups, the outfits started their descent. It was only 8:00 a.m. but the temperature was already approaching ninety degrees atop these Big Horn Mountains where the air was thin and the sun's rays burning. Exposed to this kind of heat for six hours, some of the meat could spoil, so, at the first aspen grove, Big Day signaled the column of trucks to stop. He instructed the men folk to make sure no pieces of the feast food touched each other. Next, he asked them to cut small branches from the white-barked trees, then layer the boughs in between and over all of the meat. Not only would this procedure keep the meat out of the hot sun and in the cool shade, but the noisy rattling and motion of the quaking aspen leaves would also deter flies and other insects from contaminating these raw provisions.

The hunting party finally returned to Pryor that evening following a lengthy sightseeing trip along Big Horn Canyon and past several historic tepee rings. The aspen boughs were removed. After eight hours of 100-degree heat, not one inch of the meat had been lost to spoilage. With knives flying and a circular saw racing, the quarters were further reduced to more manageable eight-pound roasts, wrapped in foil and thrown into the freezer to await the feast, now two weeks away.

Sweats and prayers continued in the ensuing time until just a few days before the Sun Dance began. It was then a journey to the Pryor Mountains was made to get the rafter poles for the lodge. Also utilized in tepee construction, lodgepole pines are favored because they are relatively straight and come in the fifty-foot lengths necessary for the roof line. They are also comparatively free of branch growth along their span except at the crown, which minimizes preparation procedures.

John Pretty On Top, an authorized Sun Dance Chief on the Crow Reservation since 1984, is called on annually to assist in the ceremony and its arrangements. He brought his special Sun Dance trailer. Actually a former telephone pole hauler, the trailer contracted or expanded depending on the length of its haul, and was perfect for the assignment. After picking up a dozen youth from St. Charles Mission in Pryor who were in the VISION Summer Program on the reservation and wanted to help out, a crew of about twenty departed for the land of the big trees and the little people, atop the Pryors.

Once in the pine forest, Heywood and John strolled through the woods with heads cocked skyward, their eyes running up and down the timbers. Speaking in Crow and pointing to one tree after another, they decided which would be just right. Twelve ceiling poles, six to eight

WITH FRED TURNSBACK STOKING THE BONFIRE, CROW SUN DANCE CHIEF JOHN PRETTY ON TOP PRAYS FOR A SUCCESSFUL GOLDEN ANNIVERSARY AT AN OUTDOOR CEREMONY SPONSORED BY HEYWOOD AND MARY LOU BIG DAY.

THE LOGGING CREW LOADS LODGEPOLE
PINES THAT WILL SERVE AS THE RAFTERS
OF THE SUN DANCE LODGE.

inches in diameter, were needed. These would connect the forked circumference uprights to the forked Center Pole. A few others would be felled
and then cut into smaller segments to join the perimeter verticals, thus
closing the Sun Dance lodge circle.

Soon the chainsaw buzzed and lodgepoles crashed to the needled
carpet of the forest floor. Each tree was pruned of its side branches except
for those at the top. Four or five crew members would then, in concert,
raise each pine, parade-march to the trailer and lower it back to the
ground. After a dozen and a half were stacked, the temporary lumberjacks
broke for a picnic lunch.

After eating, the bunch assembled around a standing lodgepole onto
which Big Day had tied his white handkerchief. His Sun Dance bag of
medicine, pipe, and *kinnikinnik*, or smoking mixture, hung from a branch
stub of a neighboring pine. This particular tree was different from the
others in that its top was forked. It would become the "chief pole," the
first rafter to be positioned. The chainsaw was now exchanged for an ax
out of respect. Heywood said a few words and, as he had done before so
many other times along this Sun Dance trail, uttered a prayer.

He removed his bandanna and then his bag. He loaded his stone pipe
with holy tobacco, stepped just about as close to the forked tree as he
could get and then lit the *kinnikinnik*. With his left hand holding the pipe
and right hand palming the trunk, Heywood continued his supplications
along with the smoke offerings. When he finished, the pipe was laid aside.

Big Day and Pretty On Top placed a hand on, and leaned into, the
chief pole. With utmost reverence, the two sang a special song just for that
tree. Though the echo of the duet was not audible, it is the Crow belief
that that sacred sound has a life of its own and will continue to reverberate
through the trees, over the mountains and along the rivers, forever.
"There is no end to it," Heywood asserted. "Maybe when the wind was

This particular tree was different from the others in that its top was forked. It would become the "chief pole," the first rafter to be positioned.

blowin' and when you were out on the hills, you can hear the singin' of the trees. They might even have to sing that same song during at the time of the [next] harvesting. That same song is still goin' 'round [The song that William Big Day sang when he cut down those lodgepoles for the 1941 Sun Dance]. It's still singin' the same song. So that's why I said there's no end to it!"

Afterward, the chief pole was smudged with sweet cedar. Big Day grabbed the ax and took the first four blows to the trunk at ground level. Pretty On Top continued with four more swings, followed by Bill, Jace and Derek. In no time, the forked pine smashed to the ground. As soon as it was trimmed, the group carted it off to the trailer. Heywood dug a little hole next to the stump, deposited the remaining contents of his pipe and covered it back up. He explained, "I gave [back] ashes on the east side of the trunk to the natural ground of Mother Earth. I'm trading. You have to give something. You just can't pick up the tree and steal it away from the mountains. So you have to give. Whatever you do, you have to give something. That's one of our beliefs. Some of these days, it'll grow another, maybe even better than the one I got."

The rafter poles were then stacked on the retractable trailer. The outside uprights were tightened while come-alongs encircled and further secured the long, hefty load. The pickup and lumber wagon threaded through the forest, out into a clearing and down the mountain road back to Pryor. Another Sun Dance task was accomplished.

Thursday, July 25, the day the Sun Dance was to begin and the morning after the last Outdoor Prayer Ceremony, Big Day rounded up about thirty men to go get the Center Pole. The Center Pole is always a forked cottonwood and, like the other poles, must be indigenous to Crow Country. Because its existence is so dependent on water (another reason for its sacred value and usage), it is usually found in the valleys alongside

MEDICINE MEN HEYWOOD BIG DAY AND JOHN PRETTY ON TOP SING A
SPECIAL SONG TO THE CHIEF POLE, THE FORKED LODGEPOLE RAFTER.

OPPOSITE PAGE: HEYWOOD BIG DAY LIGHTS HOLY TOBACCO IN THE PEACE PIPE AND
PRAYS TO AKBAATATDÍA PRIOR TO CHOPPING DOWN THE COTTONWOOD CENTER POLE.

streams and rivers or within root-range of the water table. Heywood had located the perfect tree about fifteen miles north of Pryor in the bottomlands of Pryor Creek.

The Center Pole is the all-important element of the Sun Dance lodge. It is the hub of the Sun Dance lodge circle. It is one with Mother Earth and supports the buffalo head, eagle, willow bundles (which deter evil spirits), flags, and tobacco pouches, and supports the dancers during the ceremony. According to Heywood, it is also the heart of the Sun Dance, and it circulates and recirculates the prayers, power and spirits ... from inside out and outside in ... circles of sacrifice, realization and strength. Once construction is complete, "the Center Pole contains all of the sacred power of the universe," asserted Tom Yellowtail, "and as the dancers concentrate on the center tree, so also do they concentrate their prayers on *Acbadadea [Akbaatatdía]*" (Yellowtail, 165).

Once the Center Pole cutting crew arrived at the site, not far from where Blue Creek Road meets Pryor Road at the T-intersection, Big Day implemented traditional standards and practices. "It's the same thing like when we were up on the mountains cuttin' that chief pole," Heywood described. "We smoked and cedared. And we have to give the tobacco on the inside of the pipe. I shared my tobacco with the rest of the boys. And so we sang a [special Center Pole] song four times. After we got done singin' the song, then I started hitting the wood with the ax and we started chopping it. I must have hit it about more than four times so I gave it to the next man. And the next man. And the next man. We've got an assembly line that's goin' through that ax. Once we got it down, we put it in the wagon and took it back to Pryor."

A four-foot-deep hole was dug where Big Day believed that first Center Pole was located in 1941. Before the cottonwood was erected, it was necessary to paint three rings (representing the three days of the Sun

Dance) around the base end of the trunk. The grey-black medium was a mixture of water and charcoal from the last Outdoor Ceremonial fire - as Heywood would say, "the real McCoy, a paint from Mother Nature and not from K Mart!" The painters were the children and Heywood could not do without their assistance, too.

"I asked them little guys," Big Day detailed, "every little child, even down to the infant, for their help. They've got more spirit than you have. The little people were the ones who did the coloring with the black charcoal around that pole. A lot of times, you've seen the little childrens were playin' with mud balls or mud pie or even building castles. Every human nature, like the people, I need all of the help that I can [get], not only by myself. If I do it myself," Big Day laughed out loud, "it won't be successful. It has to be all of the people, as well as the children."

While the Center Pole was still down, Big Day adorned its two divergent branches. Onto what would be the north fork, he placed a white cloth offering, or flag, signifying the earth, daylight and purity. Onto what would be the south fork, he tied a blue banner that represented a cloudless sky (for which they hoped), the heavens and the night. Just above the prayer cloths, Heywood fastened a pouch of Bull Durham tobacco. "This is for the safe journey and the good weather and to have the good Spirit in the Sun Dance lodge, to have a good power that we could heal the people and take off the problems that they have," he said.

With all of the symbolic offerings on the Y-shaped tree, the time had come to raise the Center Pole. Fifty men gathered up and down the cottonwood, half of them on each side. Big Day started singing the "Tree Song." Others in the group who knew it joined in. They sang it four times.

Originally from Shoshone country, the "Tree Song" pays homage to an animate cottonwood whose spirit is very much alive. The song enables the men to transfer their spiritual energy to real strength, the Center Pole

Felice, Elisha and Randolph Big Day, Heywood and Mary Lou's grandkids, paint the three black rings around the center pole.

becoming lighter each time the song is sung. The men bent down, grabbed the pole and lifted it up to about waist level before returning it to the ground. They sang the song four more times, then repeated the up-down Center Pole procedure. The entire process was enacted a total of four times when, on the last, the tree gradually went up.

By the hole, the base of the Center Pole was resting on a round log that would roll. A rope had been tied to each fork and was manned, pulled, and steered by several individuals to the east. From the west, several men held two pairs of long poles with a sling at the opposite end pushing up on each fork. Soon the Center Pole was raised to about a seventy-degree angle, rolled on the log, and dropped into the hole. The rope crews pulled and finely tuned the tops so that the opening of the fork was on an east-west axis while the forks themselves were on a north-south line.

Once the tree was just right, the men returned dirt to the hole and tamped it down around the pole. Now that the tree was again one with Mother Earth, the men's physical strength was transformed back into spiritual joy, completing the heavenly circuit. To Heywood, raising the Center Pole with everyone pitching in to help was akin to friends giving a hand to the elderly, to the weak, to the sick so that they, too, may stand.

Now came the time to align the twelve forked vertical poles that would, when connected, form the exterior circular wall of the lodge. Some medicine men have used cottonwood; others prefer box elder. But Heywood selected aspen because of its beautiful white bark and availability. Several uprights were donated and a crew harvested the remainder. When it came time to plant the aspens along the perimeter, it turned out that three were too short. One more quick trip to the mountains would be required. Son William Big Day volunteered to go and took a couple of buddies with him. He wondered if there would be time enough to get everything done.

As Billy drove his tawny brown pickup over the rock-laced road to the foothills, he thought about how frustrating it was to have to re-do a job. He was running short on sleep, short on energy and long on chores. He had made a vow to Heywood to help in any way—to work on the outside to make sure the Sun Dance was successful while his dad and older brother, Derek, toiled on the inside. Billy had been meditating all week, asking for more time and greater strength to get all of the tasks accomplished. Now, one had to be done all over.

At a stand of aspens, William called on the First Maker, "A man needs energy to work on something like this. How do I earn it? How do I visualize all of this stuff? How do I know you're receiving my prayers?" They measured and cut two of the needed three trees. The other fellows carried the huge logs, extra-long this time, back to the pickup. It was hot, and Bill was tired, weak, sweaty and hungry.

"While they were gone, I started praying again," Billy said. "You know, it's just in the blood of being a Native American or Crow person. 'Great Spirit, I don't know if you're hearin' my prayers or not.' So I went to the last one, you know, and started cutting. After I cut it down, I turned around and here was the body of a golden eagle, all twelve tail feathers, both wings which contained the whistle bones, and the skull was even laying right there. After all of that depression I'd gone through, it all disappeared. Soon, there was a little rain drizzle came over, you know, sort of like cools down 'cause that day was like ninety-eight or 100 degrees and that little rain drizzle came over. That felt like it was a real blessing. After that, I got my strength back. That was a very huge experience for me to understand about my grandfather's Fiftieth Anniversary that we were having. It was a very mystic way!"

By the time they returned to camp with a re-energized Billy, nine of the aspen uprights had been planted around the circumference with their forks facing the Center Pole. Shortly the three replacements were in

HEYWOOD BIG DAY TRIMS EXCESS BRANCHES OFF THE TOP OF CENTER POLE PRIOR TO FASTENING PRAYER CLOTHS AND POUCHES OF TOBACCO TO THE TWO FORKS.

position. Next, teams of workers hauled the rafter poles to their respective locations. First to be set was the chief pole, which ran along the west-east axis from what would become the rear of the lodge (where Big Day and Pretty On Top would reside) to the center cottonwood. The second ceiling poles to be arranged were the pair that edged the only entrance to the lodge, an eastern opening that would enable the dancers to view the sunrise. The remaining rafters were then put in place.

Thursday afternoon was half-gone and there was plenty of work left. Some folks cut lodgepoles and nailed them from aspen to aspen, connecting the outer ring of uprights. Others fetched hundreds of aromatic fir trees and leaned them up against the perimetrical frame, forming a wall of shade and privacy, yet open enough to permit ventilation. From the bed of a pickup, John hung the buffalo mount, eagle, and two evil-repelling willow bundles from the Center Pole. Others cleaned the floor of the lodge, where participants would be dancing barefoot until Sunday.

Thomas Yellowtail, senior Crow medicine man and retired Sun Dance Chief, explained the design of the sacred lodge circle. "The upright poles form the sacred circle," he stated, "representing the spiritual reality of our tribe. The rafter poles link the sacred circle to the Center Pole, which is the sacred point where all three worlds are connected (symbolized by the three black rings): the physical world of the tribe; the spiritual world of our Medicine Fathers; and the pure world of *Acbadadea[Akbaatatdia]*. There are other meanings also. The lodge is round, and that represents the earth, which is round. The twelve poles, leading from each forked pole to the center, represent the twelve months of the year. The twelve months represent another circle, because in it we are brought back to a new beginning. The drum which we use to help carry our songs to *Acbadadea [Akbaatatdia]* is also round. All things in Nature's way are round " (Yellowtail, 150). Not to be overlooked, the sun, moon, fire pit, tepee, sweat

"The lodge is round, and that represents the earth, which is round. The twelve poles, leading from each forked pole to the center, represent the twelve months of the year. The twelve months represent another circle, because in it we are brought back to a new beginning."

— *Thomas Yellowtail*

lodge, and trunk of a [Center Pole] tree are also circular.

Because the Crow Sun Dance is non-denominational and individualistic, a person can prepare in whatever fashion is particularly appropriate. Some, like Marshall Lefthand of Lodge Grass, fasted a day or two before they got into the lodge where they began the "official" Sun Dance abstinence from food and water. Others go without sexual relations for a few days prior to the ceremony because they feel that sex diminishes their preparedness and saps their energy. The only condition which requires the individual not to enter the lodge is when a woman is in her "moon cycle" (i.e. menstruating).

Heywood had his own customized training program. "I'm gonna use all of my energy. It's gonna be hard work," he detailed. "So I prepared for my physical and for my strength and for my mind and for the spiritual side. I was prepared. Just before I go in, I even, myself, I even went in the sweat lodge for four times, strictly for that reason. I know I was prepared. Then what I like to do about one or two hours before goin' in, I sure like to drink that broth soup [the same substance that he first consumed right after his infant life was spared]. I sure like that. Some reason that it feels like the taste, it goes all the way up to the second day as well as the third day."

As the light of day was sinking toward the west, dancers began to get dressed for the procession into the lodge and the start-up of the Sun Dance. The men were usually bare-chested and wore hand-sewn skirts that hung from the waist to the ground, with a sash covering the waistline. Women were attired in homemade dresses, many times of a floral pattern. Each wore an eagle bone whistle, which dangled from a leather thong around his/her neck. All held eagle plumes in each hand which, when not used, hung from a cord fastened to their little fingers. No one wore shoes out of respect for the sacred Sun Dance circle; only naked, humble feet could come in contact with the holy "church" floor. Many had richly

John Pretty On Top
readies the buffalo
mount before it is hung
on the Center Pole.

colored Pendleton or Hudson Bay blankets draped over their shoulders. As the golden sun neared the rolling western horizon and was about to give its goodnight kiss to comfort the earth, the Sun Dancers gathered at the rear of the lodge near the fire of the fourth Outdoor Ceremonial (which had taken place a mere twenty-four hours earlier) and formed two long lines, men toward the front, women at the rear.

Big Day and Pretty On Top arrived. Each took his place in the lead of one of the lines. When the last speck of sun disappeared, Heywood and John inaugurated the proceedings by trilling on their whistles. Instantly the other 102 Sun Dancers joined in on their instruments, piercing the air with countless, high-pitched tones that seemed to urge on the participants and spectators. The two leaders then embarked on a march in opposite directions around the periphery of the lodge. When Heywood's counter-clockwise line encountered John's clockwise route at the entrance the first time, Big Day kept to the inside track. The second time they met, they entered through the east doorway and took their places along the wall.

Once everyone was inside and in place, the whistles of the eagle went still. The Golden Anniversary Crow Sun Dance was now under way.

Phil Beaumont summoned the families, friends and supporters to bring the dancers' bedding and minimal supplies to the entrance. As each bedroll was identified, Beaumont called out the dancer's name to come fetch his or her sleeping bag. Their three-day compartments were now furnished with the bare necessities. Gordon Plain Bull set up his drum, sat down with his singers and sang four Sun Dance songs. During each song, Heywood approached the Center Pole with his pipe, offering prayer smoke and communicating with *Akbaatatdia*. These holy petitions were similar to those uttered at the first Medicine Bundle Ceremony seven months earlier.

Before the fourth song was finished, Big Day moved close to the sacred cottonwood tree and began trilling on his eagle bone whistle. The other

Sun Dancers joined him at the hub and whistled on their eagle bones. At this point the dancing officially began. Head firetender Fred Turnsback kindled a blaze that cut through the growing darkness and kept pace with the participants, who danced without rest until three o'clock in the morning. On the first night, Sun Dancers are expected to dance as long as the singers keep drumming; on subsequent nights, the reverse is true, with the dancers controlling the duration of the music.

The fire was fed throughout the night until after the "Sunrise Ceremony" the next morning. With so much spiritual excitement in the air and adrenaline in the heart, the Sun Dancers got less than two hours of sleep that first night. Twenty minutes before the sun christened Friday, the camp crier awakened those inside. Soon they were rising from their stations, milling about in bare feet, trying to insulate their bodies from the pre-light chill with Pendleton blankets wrapped around themselves. Big Day, Yellowtail, Pretty On Top, and another assistant, John Cummins, took their positions by the fire circle (one-third of the way between the door and the Center Pole) and sat down facing the east. The other dancers assembled alongside and behind them in a multi-tiered crescent. Observers were not permitted to stand in the entrance because they would block the view of the ascending sun during this special service.

Plain Bull and his drummers initiated the "Sunrise Song." This particular "Sunrise Song" originally belonged to William Big Day and was then passed down to Heywood. It is a song of praise to "Old Man Sun," acknowledging that his spirit is coming up over the horizon. Through their singing, participants addressed, needed, and received the spiritual power of the sun. They concurrently started to "whistle up the sun" on their wing bones. The blend of 100-plus high-pitched whistles and the deep monotonal resonance of bass drum was a unique, emotional amalgam of sound, one that would not be forgotten for a long time to come,

Head firetender Fred Turnsback kindled a blaze that cut through the growing darkness and kept pace with the participants, who danced without rest until three o'clock in the morning.

even by those who were observing. Gordon attested to the power of the moment, "When you sing that 'Sunrise Song,' it really brings the Spirit into that Sun Dance. That song, it's really sacred to us. We respect it."

As the sun broke over the horizon and the first rays bathed the dancers in red-orange light, they extended their arms eastward, drew their hands back to their bodies and then symbolically "washed" the sun's positive influence all over themselves. When the sun was fully risen, the whistles, voices and drum ceased. The Sun Dancers seated themselves and sang each of four songs four times. After each one, the participants blew their whistles four times. While some practices of the Sun Dance were open to personal interpretation, the Sunrise Service was rigidly traditional with certain necessary formalities.

SUSPENDED FROM A RAFTER AND THE CENTER POLE, THE BALD EAGLE AND BUFFALO AWAIT THE ARRIVAL OF THE SUN DANCERS.

The recurring, sacred number "four" permeates all levels of Indian culture and, in particular, reaches into every corner of Crow life. Big Day explains that the initial perception of the holiness of "four" was conceived centuries ago while a warrior prayed in the middle of the night during a vision quest. Facing the east in darkness at 4:00 a.m., the Crow fixed his sight on the Morning Star and petitioned the First Maker for four prayer wishes. The Indian's response came when the four-pronged Morning Star twinkled four different colors, alternately sparkling in red, green, yellow and white. During each of the four seasons, the four flickering hues of the Morning Star changed to four other colors.

The number four occurs in other aspects of Crow life as well. Four directions complete a full circle. Four main poles are lashed together to begin raising a tepee. A sweat bath, or little lodge, is comprised of four rounds of water pouring. Prior to a Crow Sun Dance, four Medicine Bundle Ceremonies are held in which four medicine men preside. Four Outdoor Ceremonies take place, at which four important sites are located. Four songs, sung four times. The Big Lodge transpires over the course of

AFTER CIRCLING OUTSIDE ONCE, THE TWO
LINES OF SUN DANCERS ENTER THE LODGE
AND BEGIN THE GOLDEN ANNIVERSARY.

four days. A vow to go into the Sun Dance is fulfilled when the pledger has completed four of the ceremonies. Four, forever. On and on!

With the dancers seated around him, Heywood stood up and moved to the fire circle, which contained the night's worth of embers. He reached into his bank deposit bag of dried cedar and sprinkled a handful of the sacred incense on the coals. The smoke and scent blessed the dancers, the lodge, the bystanders on the outside, the entire Sun Dance encampment and beyond. Next, Big Day prayed to the Almighty for the Sun Dance, for those dancing, for the Crow people, for Indians across the country and for all of humanity. With tears welling up in his eyes, Heywood invoked the One Divine Being to answer the dancers' petitions for the alleviation of pain, suffering and sickness, for the successful attainment of personal goals and for the continued protection of family members and friends in critical situations.

Thereafter the Sunrise Ceremony was officially concluded. The firetender came back into the lodge, scooped some coals from the fire into his shovel, and took them to the periphery outside the lodge. Repeating this routine several times, he scattered a half-dozen small fires about so that all people present could smudge themselves with cedar. The dancers joined their supporters outside the lodge for a few minutes of visitation, rest and relaxation. Then they returned to their stations for a couple of hours of naps and/or introspection before the day's dancing began, signaled by the beat of the drum.

Gordon Plain Bull, Heywood's brother-in-law, was the drum chief in charge of the music. It was his responsibility to make sure there were four or five groups of singers who could take turns rotating drum duty. Plain Bull has been drumming and singing for over forty years, ever since, as a six-year-old boy, he started beating on an inverted washtub while singing newly learned Sun Dance songs. At seventeen, he danced in the ceremony himself and kept his vow to go in four times. Having been both a participant and drummer, Gordon knows that the drum is the heartbeat of the Sun Dance, and singing the powerful accompaniment. "This singin' really helps the dancers," Plain Bull professed. "They give you that peace pipe, you smoke it and then you pray with it. You pray to the Almighty to bring good songs for the dancers, spiritual songs. The drum helps to bring that Spirit into that lodge and into the good songs—spirited, lively songs to help the dancers."

Around 11:00 a.m., Gordon entered the lodge with his bass drum and five other singers. Unfolding their personalized chairs, they set up in the southern portion of the entryway, just inside. Plain Bull initiated the beat and established the pace while the others joined in. Big Day had requested this specific Sun Dance song for the start because it was special; it was his own. Three more songs followed. On the fifth, the dancers swung into motion, running to the Center Pole and blowing their whistles and prayers heavenward. With eyes still fixed on the buffalo, eagle or some other focal point on the cottonwood, they would dance backwards to their stations. Of course, the participants knew most of the Sun Dance songs, many of which contained non-verbal vocalizations, and knew when to hustle to the tree and then return to the perimeter.

As in other patriarchal cultures of the past, women have not always been permitted to enter the Sun Dance.

Sometimes, the Sun Dancers would remain at the Center Pole and have a prayer smoke. With one hand on the trunk, they prayed to the Great Spirit on the fumes of holy tobacco and exchanged weakness for strength by completing the "circuit" at the all-powerful Center Pole, their conduit to the heavens. When they were done, they extinguished their cigarettes by sticking them into the powdered dirt at the base of the tree. They then danced backwards, at the proper interval, to their stations.

As in other patriarchal cultures of the past, women have not always been permitted to enter the Sun Dance. Some might fast on the outside, but from 1941 until the early 1960s there were no female dancers. Following some all-women Shoshone Sun Dances at Bannock Creek, Idaho, in the late 1950s, Rainbow and William Big Day took steps to blend the ceremony on their own reservations by merging the two separate Sun Dances into an integrated affair.

Clara Rides Horse Smells, from Pryor, has been dancing in the Big Lodge for twenty-five years and was one of those pioneering women. She has participated in a Sun Dance every year since she first went in, and during some summers has danced two or three times. She practices what she believes and believes she has received prayer answers and witnessed enough outright miracles to substantiate her convictions.

Clara was originally inspired to go in after she got word, one night in 1967, that her sister was in a California hospital with kidney failure and had only forty-eight hours to live. Clara told her brother-in-law over the phone, "What I want you to do now is roll a tobacco and face the sun in the morning. Right before the sun rises, I want you to kneel down and pray. After you're done praying, put your cigarette down, not on the pavement. I want you to put it on the ground, in the dirt or it would be even better if you put it by a tree. You do that for four mornings. [If she's still alive on the] Fourth morning, put a little water in a cup and pray over it. Take it to her and let her drink it."

Smells prayed to *Akbaatatdía* from Pryor and made the vow that if her sister lived, she would go into the Sun Dance. The sister got better, was eventually released from the hospital and returned to a normal life. Clara kept her promise and entered the Big Lodge at Crow Agency for the first time in 1968, clutching only a Pendleton blanket, some tobacco, sweetgrass and sage. That was over thirty Sun Dances ago, including several Lakota-style flesh-piercing ceremonies.

Clara's testimonial did not stop there. Her son dove into a shallow irrigation ditch and struck his head on some submerged concrete blocks. His scalp was peeled off the skull from neck to forehead and he blew out several spinal column discs. His doctors prognosticated that he would never be active, never play sports. As she always did, Clara went back into the Sun Dance. "I asked the Creator," Smells prayed, " 'I want my son to become a [whole] man. I want him to do everything by himself so that he can go hunting or horseback or play basketball or football.' The Creator answered my prayers!" In 1983, her son played for Plenty Coups High School at the state basketball championships in Great Falls ... and won.

The drumming and singing, dancing and whistling continued under the blistering summer sun. The air was filled with high-pitched trills, low-toned throbs and the quiet urgency of shuffling feet. Participants rushed from their stations to the Center Pole and back again in a blur, soaked with the sweat of their single-minded motion. The more serious participants went almost non-stop because they knew that only through prayer, dehydration, exhaustion, hyperventilation and personal sacrifice would they receive a vision from the First Maker through the Medicine Fathers. By mid-afternoon, the Nighthawk Singers from Lodge Grass had rotated in to strike the drum, relieving Plain Bull and his chorus, whose voices were going hoarse. Throughout the afternoon, evening and night, the dancers' energies were expended without pause. As long as there was one dancer in motion, the singers continued to beat the heart of the Sun Dance.

The second day, Saturday, was plump with activity. After "whistling up the sun" at the Sunrise Ceremony and the special prayers by Big Day and Yellowtail, the dancers left the lodge to join their supporters on the outside. When they were done smudging themselves with sweet cedar on this morning, they tracked down their clan uncles, medicine men or other spiritual leaders who had the right or power to paint the dancer with the painter's particular Sun Dance color and design. Not just anyone did the

As long as there was one dancer in motion, the singers continued to beat the heart of the Sun Dance.

Trilling through eagle bone whistles,
104 Sun Dancers pray to the One
Divine Being at the Sunrise Service.

painting; only an exceptional individual with distinctive medicine and/or privilege was permitted to paint a Sun Dancer. In so doing, the dancer was preparing for a sacred battle with the buffalo hung on the Center Pole ... an internal, spiritual war.

Before the bison was mounted to the tree, its face had also been painted with a white clay-water mix. This represented what the buffalo did in his natural surroundings before he locked horns with an adversary: he pawed at the ground, stirred up some dust, maybe even thrashed around in it. Yellowtail related, "When the buffalo is roaming out in the prairies, he decorates himself with dirt. It is a medicine the buffalo creates by rolling in the dust and whipping it up. He always does this before a battle. He is going to war, and he prepares himself by making medicine and painting " (Yellowtail, 152). And from the bison, as well as from other animals, Indians learned to paint themselves, to dance and to derive holy medicine from their natural world.

When the dancers returned to the lodge, a flag service was held. The two blue and white Sun Dance flags flew proudly during the entire ceremony ... and, for that matter, as long as the Center Pole would stand. On the morning of this second day, the American flag was hoisted in military fashion on a lodgepole pine to the left of the entrance. Chris Comes Up donated the use of his dad's burial flag. As it was raised, Plain Bull and the drummers sang the Sun Dance "Flag Song" (different from a powwow flag song rendition) as everyone present stood at attention. For this special day, the American flag waved in the Pryor Mountain breezes.

The second day was also the time when many significant personal spiritual events took place. First, 105 debarked saplings were brought in and anchored between each compartment. Dug into the ground at the bottom and fastened at the top to the interior frame of the lodge, they provided a handhold for the increasingly weary dancers. Big Day called these poles "canes" because of their metaphorical connection to the canes old people often have to use to stand up and get around. "These canes," Heywood remarked, "represent for our lives, for the history of the life that you want to see your grandchildren for about four or five or six generations. In other words, you want to live a long time." A continuous line of willows was tied to the tops of the canes, connecting all and creating a circle of protection to discourage evil spirits from entering the lodge.

In addition, an even larger ring of support circumscribed the Sun Dance lodge at the *Itta'tbachiash* [William Big Day's Crow Indian name] Ceremonial Grounds. Because the Golden Anniversary Big Lodge was the center of reservation life for those four days, hundreds of family members and friends "moved" to Pryor to aid, abet and assist their loved ones—physically and emotionally—through this revelational experience. Tepees, wall tents, campers, trailers and even sleeping bags under the stars created a huge outermost concentric ring around the Center Pole. Airborne dust trails followed the cars and trucks that crossed Pryor Creek on the solitary dirt road to the historic Big Day Big Lodge. People drifted in from their camps to the Sun Dance, then on to other encampments for reunions or visits. Off-reservation visitors wandered aimlessly until they were invited into a camp for a Crow welcome and some refreshments. Joyous hours of socializing took place over copious amounts of coffee.

To prepare for what lay ahead, supporters from the outside brought in props and aids to benefit the participants. The dancers received armfuls of cool, moisture-laden cattails with which they would cover their beds, creating a comfortable, refreshing place to rest. They were also given bunches of sweet sage and horsemint, natural aromas which would be hung around their stalls to soothe and alleviate the suffering (as well as hopefully cover up any cooking smells drifting through the lodge from the neighboring camps). Outsiders contributed packs of menthol cigarettes to

THE SUN DANCERS "CHALLENGE THE
BUFFALO" BY RUNNING OR DANCING TO
THE CENTER POLE, AND THEN BACK TO
THEIR STALLS.

the dancers and made special prayer requests.

After all of the preliminaries were completed, the second day's dancing resumed, and intensified. Saturday's heat was extreme, with temperatures in the upper nineties. The dancers were tired, hot, famished, dry, hurting and primed for a momentous signal, a prominent vision. Racing up to the Center Pole, rapidly reversing directions back to their cubbyholes, huffing and puffing on their eagle whistles, praying on the whiffs of tobacco smoke, abstaining from food and water, many Sun Dancers were on the verge of experiencing what they had come for in the first place. In the words of Bill Big Day, who had been in several Sun Dances himself, "they have that Dancing Spirit."

Nearing this dreamlike state, the dancer, staring into the eyes of the bison for the past forty hours, sees a buffalo that is not only alive but a full-bodied beast charging him/her. The sweet sage hanging from each nostril symbolizes the breath, the snorting and the fervor of battle. "When these buffalo are charging," Heywood explained, "you see their nostrils were red and you seen some white stuff comin' out of him. While we were three days and three nights of that, we were challenging him so that once he gets mad, he'll give us the power."

The Sun Dancers continued to press on towards that steep precipice, charging and challenging the buffalo. "They knew the chances of getting something 'good' increased when a dancer kept going. Suddenly he might see the buffalo come to life or a herd of them coming to 'run over him.' Other dancers, sensing the imminence of power, exerted more effort, and the drummer-singers increased the tempo and sang without letup. He must dance right up to the tree if he were to get the power." (Voget, 268).

From where he sat facing the interior of the lodge, Drum Chief Plain Bull had one eye on a swaying dancer and the other on Big Day. It was obvious that this person had the "Dancing Spirit," and by the way he was weaving outside his path, he was pushing himself to the limit. The Sun Dance song could not stop until he dropped. "It was that first song we sang after I prayed with that pipe," Plain Bull said. "It took us three and one-half hours to sing that one song, three and one-half hours! That power hit one guy, one guy, and that's why it took us three and one-half hours to sing that one song. You look at the dancers and if some are going to fall or get the power, you can't stop when there's something like that goin'. That's why we sang for three and one-half hours!"

The young man finally "took a fall" and collapsed on the ground. In his vision, and according to Crow interpretation, the buffalo had hooked the dancer with his horns and tossed him up into the air. He was now unconscious, deep in his vision; fellow dancers quickly covered him up with a white sheet. His spirit was receiving instructions concerning his new medicine, its manifestations and its future use. His gift from the Sun Dance had finally come.

It was alarming for spectators who did not know what was going on to witness a Sun Dancer not only tumble to the ground, but also to see him left in the hot sun while the ceremony continued. They did not understand that it was of great benefit when this happened, that it was one of the intended results of going into a Sun Dance. The man was merely in a deep sleep for a few minutes and was being blessed with spiritual rewards—power, communications, medicine and/or directions, which, when realized and acted upon, would help him, other Crow people, or the Tribe.

An Anglo visitor asked Heywood if he had ever witnessed an unconscious dancer having to be hospitalized. With a proud grin and a short chuckle to the obviously "white" question, Big Day responded, "Of all these years that I have gone down to the Sun Dance—and I've seen many of them—I haven't seen anyone of them that's in the lodge that has had to go into the hospital. The powerful medicine man or Sun Dance Chief has

His spirit was receiving instructions concerning his new medicine, its manifestations and its future use. His gift from the Sun Dance had finally come.

always been able to deal with anything, or 'doctor' someone who has needed help."

Clara Rides Horse Smells even witnessed an old woman dying in the Big Lodge. The lady, who had danced many times in the ceremony, plunged to the ground and literally quit breathing. The medicine man rushed to her side, doctored her pulseless body, and shortly revived her back to life. Not only was the Sun Dance a place of worship, a source of omnipotent power and strength, but also a Plains Indian 'hospital' where the sick and infirm came to be healed.

Many Crows, as well as non-Crows on the outside, had afflictions and wanted to be treated by either Big Day, Pretty On Top or Cummins. Saturday afternoon was the time for this. Supporters and spectators took off their shoes at the lodge entrance and formed a prayer line, or healing line. In turn, they made their way barefoot across the holy ground to the Center Pole. After telling one of the medicine men his problem, the patient placed his hands on the tree where the sacred power of the universe was currently concentrated. The medicine man began to pray for the patient and then doctor him from head to toe with medicine feathers. He first "recharged" his fan on the Center Pole, touched the site of the ailment and then "drew out" the problem through the sacred plumage. The illness was immediately cast to the east where the four winds dispersed it to nothingness. When the doctoring was complete, patient offered medicine man a small gift of sage, cedar, or tobacco and, in so doing, thanked the Great Spirit for his benevolence.

Later that afternoon, storm clouds moved into Crow Country. The blue skies darkened to gray and the overcast began to look more ominous. The good news was that this cooled things off and made it easier for the dancers. The bad news was that it looked like rain was imminent and that the participants might soon have to slosh through mud to the Center Pole.

ON THE SECOND DAY, A RAINSTORM PASSED
THROUGH PRYOR VALLEY AND SATURATED
EVERYTHING...EXCEPT THE SACRED SUN DANCE
LODGE AND ITS INHABITANTS.

Worse yet, if thunder and lightning encroached, as they often do at this time of the year, it would become quite dangerous out here in the flats of Pryor Valley. The peaks of the nearby mountains were now shrouded in a charcoal layer of thunderheads that stretched all around the horizon. The darker diagonal stripes of rain could be seen not far off in all directions.

Mick Fedullo, an Indian education consultant and author who lives in Pryor, attended the Golden Anniversary Crow Sun Dance as a spectator, assistant outside the lodge and eyewitness to what transpired. "There were storms all around, clouds brewing up. It was a concern for everyone," he said. "One of the things I noticed was that, as I looked around, there were storm clouds all around us, all around Pryor in the valley. Then when I looked up in the sky, right overhead, the sky was completely blue. It was like a blue circle above us, just about centered over the Sun Dance lodge. And uh, aaah, aish! I just really remember being affected by that emotionally and watching and waiting to see what was going to happen. It was an amazing thing to witness because you could see the rain coming down all around us. And yet it was kind of like a donut of storm around the Sun Dance area, and it never rained on us. The storms never came over the Sun Dance lodge, the rains never came there. We were blessed with that opening over the lodge."

Though Big Day humbly declined to comment about what happened, or about his particular role in this mystical incident, it is a matter of public record that both Rainbow and Yellowtail, when circumstances dictated, with the help and power of *Akbaatatdía*, have "split the clouds."

About the time the storms passed and the skies cleared, Mary Lou asked the boys to get started on the underground barbeque. A traditional Indian method for cooking large amounts of meat, this subterranean oven utilizes heat, moisture and the flavor of the earth itself to slowly roast the meat—in this case, two buffalo and one cow. It was Saturday evening and

It is a matter of public record that both Rainbow and Yellowtail, when circumstances dictated, with the help and power of Akbaatatdía, *have "split the clouds."*

the post-Sun Dance feast was less than twenty-four hours away.

Junior and Bill Big Day recruited a couple of buddies to help them dig a hole fifteen yards above Pryor Creek. With shovels flashing and dirt flying, the crew managed to excavate a seven-foot-square, five-foot-deep cavity in short order. A pickup load of firewood was dumped into the crater and torched. They would now have to wait several hours until all of the wood burned down to a bed of embers. With time on their hands and exhaustion filling their bodies, the young men decided to go into the Little (sweat) Lodge.

The sweat fire heated up the stones, and the lodge pit to the right of the doorway was loaded with two dozen hot rocks. (Billy entered first because, as the one who had the "right" to officiate, he would do the "pouring.") One by one, the other young men crawled into the sweat and took their positions in the ten-foot-diameter dome. A steel bucket of steaming water and dipper were placed inside. The many-blanket-thick flap was pulled down over the entrance and the confines of this Indian church went black except for the red-orange glow emanating from the pit. Big Day ladled water over the rocks, praying in Crow. The sizzling and popping of liquid converting to steam contrasted with the Sun Dance sounds of drum, songs and whistles just across the stream. However, the supplications that rose out of this Little Lodge were basically the same as those that ascended from the Big Lodge.

Into the second round of the sweat, more prayers were said, and the four men lay in a state of ultimate relaxation—naked, exhausted, prone and comfortably hot in pitch darkness. Spirituality had never been quite so soothing. "Willie was sitting right by me," Bill recalled, "and he was talking. Later on, I heard him and he was snoring. All of a sudden, the other guys were all snoring. Everyone was snoring and I was the only one [who wasn't]. I picked up my dipper and filled it up with water again. I was

DURING THE SUNRISE CEREMONY,
HEYWOOD BIG DAY PRAYS TO THE RISING
SUN AND TO AKBAATATDÍA FOR THE SUN
DANCERS, CROW PEOPLE, INDIANS ACROSS
THE COUNTRY AND ALL HUMANITY.

so tired and listening to them snoring that I started falling asleep, too.

"After we were sleeping for hours," Bill continued, "I had my dipper of water [and thus his hand] over the hot rocks. The part where it woke me up was when my hands were burning and I started hollering, you know, 'Aaaaaaa!' That must have woke Willie and he started yelling. Then everyone started screaming, scarin' each other in the dark."

Once they got themselves cool, calm and collected, the cooking committee members realized they had been in the sweat lodge three times the normal duration but completed only half of of the usual four rounds. They exited the Little Lodge, took a refreshing swim in Pryor Creek, dressed and returned to the world of responsibilities and chores.

The group checked the barbeque pit to find that the flames had ebbed and two feet of gleaming coals remained, perfect for the underground oven. They placed several bed springs on top of the embers to serve as a gigantic grill. Approximately seventy-five foil-wrapped roasts were positioned on the grates. Then they layered sheets of corrugated metal over the meat before spading the dirt back into the hole.

As the night passed its midpoint, one Sun Dancer continued to charge the buffalo. The drummers pounded and sang as a lone eagle bone whistle sailed from its perch to the Center Pole and back, searching for that holy destination. Most of the participants lay motionless on their cattail cots. A few were still awake, watching the solitary figure trying to reach his mystical plateau. It would not happen tonight. Finally acknowledging it, he returned to his stall for much-needed rest.

The next morning, all 104 spiritual contributors gathered around the fire circle under mauve clouds for the customary Sunrise Ceremony. Dancers zealously whistled up the sun. John Cummins smudged these last-day proceedings with nature's incense. Yellowtail, Pretty On Top and Big Day invoked *Akbaatatdia's* blessings on every man, woman and child in

58

the world. It was ironic that this Fiftieth Anniversary Crow Sun Dance would culminate on a Sunday, a day on which millions of Christians also congregated to supplicate and give thanks. In fact, some of those Christian worshippers were in this Sun Dance lodge for the past three days (the same length of time between Jesus' crucifixion and his resurrection), fasting, suffering and praying to the Great Spirit.

A good many Sun Dancers do not see their individual native beliefs as an exclusive form of worship. One can be a member of an institutionalized religion as well as a Sun Dancer. Native Plains religion is not a restrictive or closed system, and many Indians combine their traditional convictions with their denominational doctrine. The late Alice Bull Tail went into the Sun Dance often but would want the Catholic priest to bring communion to her in the lodge. Another elder would take his rosary into the ceremony.

Old man (a description of respect and admiration) John Cummins, a former Crow Tribal Chairman, was a faithful Catholic parishioner as well as a Sun Dance Chief whom Big Day assisted on several occasions. For him (and others), the twelve rafter poles not only represented the months of the annual circle but also stood for Christ's twelve apostles. At his Big Lodge, Cummins hung a "little man" effigy on the Center Pole. Asked what this symbolized, he simply responded, "There was another man that was nailed to a tree!"

One white man with mixed persuasions is Father Randolph Graczyk, a Catholic priest on the Crow Reservation since 1970. Originally serving as pastor of the Lodge Grass parish, he is now the priest at St. Charles Mission in Pryor. He has been adopted by Bernard and Gloria Cummins, and made a vow, in 1972, to go into the Sun Dance if their two-month-young, dying grandson survived.

In 1973 Father Randolph became the first Catholic priest to go into a Crow Sun Dance. Since then he has participated in the ceremony six times,

As long as a single dancer continues to pursue the "spirit," the singers continue to strike the heartbeat of the Sun Dance.

receiving positive personal reinforcement on every occasion. He wanted to go into the Golden Anniversary Sun Dance but, because of the large number of Indians who wanted to go in, instead offered physical and spiritual help to his dear friends in the Big Day family from outside the lodge.

Shedding light on the Sun Dance and his unique association with it, Father Randolph declared, "A motivation on my part was looking in the past, the Catholic Church was involved—along with the government and schools and everything—in attempting to suppress Indian culture. I felt that my taking part in these things (i.e. Little Lodge, Big Lodge, Native American Church, etc.) would begin to show that the Church now respects Native Americans and their ways of prayer."

Native Plains religion is not a restrictive or closed system, and many Indians combine their traditional convictions with their denominational doctrine.

"In an Indian religious ceremony," he continued, "it's the ritual of actual activity that is foremost. I think people can come to the ceremony with quite different belief systems and as long as they commit themselves to doing everything in the right way, their particular theological framework doesn't really matter that much. I go in as a believing Catholic."

Graczyk's insightful perspective is enhanced by his own experiences. "The experience of praying for people and being prayed for meant a lot to me," he explained. "It's a very intense experience of community also, I think, in a Sun Dance. There's a sense of community, in that you're all in this together. You're taken out of your everyday life and put into this lodge, which is like its own world for three days. You're all dressed the same. You're all doing the same things. You're suffering and praying together and, to me, that's one of the key things about this Sun Dance. There are singers, people on the outside, helping and supporting, painters and more. It's not only vertical, it's also horizontal. It's a real community experience of bringing people together in a common spiritual effort."

At the Golden Anniversary Sun Dance, the sphere of support even extended past the Sun Dance grounds ... and beyond. Roosting high on a foothill point overlooking Pryor Valley sat the miniscule figure of a white man, in white skirt, who had journeyed from Pennsylvania to participate in this historical Sun Dance. As it was, there were more dancing Indians than space, and the lodge had to be expanded by shrinking the entrance. The Anglo was turned away because there was no room. Nevertheless, he joined in with his fasting, dancing, prayers and presence from a distance to the southwest, still close enough to hear the drumming, singing and whistling emanating from the lodge.

Farther away still, beyond the borders of Montana, sixteen Catholic nuns from Indiana and twenty sisters from Seattle fasted and prayed their way through the vigil with Big Day. Non-Catholic backers dotted Indian Country throughout the United States.

As the noon hour on Sunday approached, the dancers knew that the end was in sight. A pickup truck backed up to within twenty yards of the entryway. Two lines of bystanders facing each other formed a corridor from the tailgate to the lodge door. When Heywood gave the cue, eight volunteers unloaded four brand-new aluminum trash cans filled with fresh water and hauled them into the lodge at each of the four cardinal directions around the Center Pole.

Next, four respected women entered the Sun Dance lodge barefooted. They had been selected and honored by Big Day to distribute the water. He described the traditional reason for having four women do this: "In the natural, natural women, they're the ones that are supposed to be feeding you. The men provide the meat and the women, they cook and, in return, they feed 'em. So anything that has to do with the Sun Dance, there's always women always in there. The reason why is that we're still standing on the *Mother* Earth and the Mother Earth planted that tree for the Center Pole. Anything that was natural was from the Mother. If it wasn't for the

Mother, we probably wouldn't even be here! Even Jesus happens to have a Mother—He came from the Mother's womb."

The last song that the drummers sing is the special "Water Song." "We sing that Water Song when they bring the water into the lodge," Gordon Plain Bull explained. "That's where the power is, right there! When you sing that Water Song and the water's right there, then you look at it. They stand there and pray. Right there, I believe in that. I believe every song I sing, to help the dancers. That song is really the powerful one."

Heywood prayed over the water, the women dispensed it around the circle. The fast was broken and the dancing finished. The Sun Dance was officially done, though it would continue going on, "like Pryor Creek water to the ocean," forever. Sighs of relief and expressions of pride could be seen on the drawn faces of the 104 Sun Dancers. Prayers, hugs, and handshakes were exchanged between those inside the lodge; they now shared a spiritual and historical tie that bound them to *Akbaatatdía*, to their newly acquired Medicine Fathers, and to Heywood Big Day.

After everyone had taken their fill of the pure spring water, Big Day and Pretty On Top stood up and signaled the other dancers to stand with them. Following the two Crow spiritual leaders, the Golden Anniversary participants marched out of the Big Lodge in the same fashion as they had entered. Families, friends and spectators waited for them on the outside, offering hearty congratulations to the weary dancers.

Heywood and John led the two lines past a novel addition to the Sun Dance. A long table had been loaded with every kind of fresh fruit: apples, oranges, melons, grapes, kiwis, and bananas. The pre-feast snack station also featured fruit juices, sodas, and more water which would quickly replenish the dancers' bodily fluids.

The refreshment counter was a new introduction, one that complemented the spiritual prominence and historical significance of this particular

The fast was broken and the dancing finished. The Sun Dance was officially done, though it would continue going on, "like Pryor Creek water to the ocean," forever.

Big Lodge Ceremony. In contrast, there was no chow line at that first Crow Sun Dance in 1941. Heywood's sisters volunteered to help out in making this special contribution to the dancers. "All my relations who pitched in," bragged Big Day, "were thinking they were not helping me enough so they set up that buffet. And I was really happy for it and I was really glad for it. I really liked it. It was terrific. That was the first time that it was happening here in the Crow Reservation. It had never happened before." Only time will tell if a new tradition was initiated.

With their offspring, in-laws and grandkids trailing behind, Heywood and Mary Lou slowly ambled back to their camp. Big Day looked as if he had lost twenty pounds and gone without sleep for a week. All he could think about was getting some more of that remarkable beef broth into his system. Both symbolic and substantial, it never failed to revive him.

The Sun Dancers once again introduced fruits and fluids to their insides, and then turned their attention to showers, streams or sweat baths, in order to immerse and cleanse their outsides. Three days of fasting and whistling was enough to dehydrate their interiors, while the hot, dusty dancing encrusted their exteriors with dirt and mineral salts. Most submerged themselves in the refreshing waters of Pryor Creek, before and after sweats in the Little Lodge. All were cool and clean when they returned to the Sun Dance grounds in a couple of hours for the traditional buffalo feast.

AFTER THE SUNRISE CEREMONY, HEYWOOD BIG DAY EXITS THE LODGE TO VISIT WITH FAMILY, FRIENDS AND OTHER SUPPORTERS.

A gold- and white-striped Fiftieth Anniversary canvas fly was pitched on the grounds. From under it the food would be served. Enticing aromas wafted about. Bill Big Day's crew unearthed a pickup load of tender roasts and unpacked them at the serving line. Mary Lou boiled the ultimate in Crow delicacies, fifty (one for each annual Sun Dance) beef tongues donated by Clara Rides Horse Smells. Barbara Lee Comes Up prepared the ribs and Indian sausage. DeAnne Round Face had made a vow for her sick

A PROUD THOUGH EX-
HAUSTED HEYWOOD AND
MARY LOU BIG DAY COUNT
THEIR BLESSINGS AT THE
CONCLUSION OF THE
SUN DANCE.

MASSIVE AMOUNTS OF FOOD WERE
SERVED TO THE MULTITUDES AT THE
FEAST FOLLOWING THE COMPLETION OF
THE SUN DANCE

little girl and contributed a sizeable tub of macaroni salad. Rhonda Horn White and Roberta Stands Over Bull had fixed nearly 600 pieces of frybread the night before. Twenty-five watermelons chilled in the creek were carved into triangular slices. Almost 700 people ate their fill at the Sun Dance feast. Though no one went away hungry, there were no leftovers!

Catching his breath, Big Day reflected on those who came from far and wide to dance in the Golden Anniversary Crow Big Lodge. "It was a tremendous ceremony. Every one of them was welcome to come in. Some of them made a vow. Some of them wanted to help me for the spiritual side. Some of them wanted to go in for four times and they wanted to finish that out with their fourth time on that particular Sun Dance."

In contrast to those who had been in the Sun Dance before, Mary Elizabeth Rondeaux Berg stood out as an exception. The Big Day Sun Dance was Mary Liz's first Big Lodge Ceremony. She had been pursuing God in the white man's world by becoming Baptist, Catholic, Jewish, Lutheran, Mormon, Pentecostal, and Seventh Day Adventist, but she found no fulfillment in any of them. She was a biker and musician, played in bars and would go out of her way to shock people. After investigating Indian spirituality, Mary Liz confessed, "I decided that, alright, I'm Native American and my church is in my own backyard. I've been everywhere else and now it's time for me to think about going in the Sun Dance."

Berg began getting herself ready after having an out-of-body experience. Her sister reinforced Mary's actions by having a similar dream in which she acted as the messenger. Miracles both great and small occurred along the way, and these convinced her she was on the right path. Berg did not own an eagle bone whistle, but three inscrutably came to her. She also admitted, "We women have to worry about our moon cycles around these times. That was one of the things that I knew would be taken care of for me. I mean, all the way to my moon cycle being drastically changed the month before to accommodate going in. I knew it! There was no denying it! How many more miracles do you need to see before you believe?! I was led. Everything worked out just so well."

Mary Liz felt that the individual testing, the thirst, the hunger, the dryness, and so much pain were a small price to pay for all of the good that resulted. "I went in expecting nothing," she declared, "but ready to give it my all. I didn't know what kind of rewards you get from it. When I came out, I knew this is where I belonged. So then, I said, 'Aho! You found my place for me.' I said, 'I'll trade You my right to drink.' I know now where I belong. It changed my life!"

Her rewards have been nothing short of amazing ... and plentiful. Since the Sun Dance, she has given birth to the baby girl she wanted for some time but could not have. Her relationships with her children have become constructive and filled with love, instead of destructive and permeated with acrimony and alienation. Seeing her example, her kids now aspire to go into the Sun Dance when the time is right. And like her great grandmother, Juanita Big Shoulder, who always wore a 1921 silver dollar on a necklace, Mary Liz donned a similar coin when she went into the Big Lodge, and to this day still wears it as a testimonial of her miraculous Sun Dance experience and her continued abstinence from alcohol.

Other supernatural wonders resulted from the power of prayer and from the strength of medicines in the 1991 Crow Sun Dance. Immediately preceding the ceremony, a white man visited Heywood, told him of his plight, and offered him tobacco. This man's daughter was in an out-of-state hospital on constant dialysis while doctors scoured the country for compatible kidneys. For eight months, the search had been intense but unsuccessful. A day before the ceremony started, shortly after Big Day smoked and prayed for the child, kidneys were unexpectedly located, shipped and immediately transplanted into her. On the second day of the

Mary Liz felt that the individual testing, the thirst, the hunger, the dryness, and so much pain were a small price to pay for all of the good that resulted.

Sun Dance, the father stood in the prayer line informing Heywood that his daughter was rejecting the kidneys and that she needed more of his holy petitions. Since prayer and spiritual medicine know no distance, Heywood resumed his supplications. Within twenty-four hours, the rejection mysteriously subsided and the patient was on the mend. Within ten days, she left the hospital and returned with her mother to Billings, and a relatively normal life.

There have been a few changes in the Sun Dance since the 1800s. Originally, the ceremony was about prayer, self-denial and suffering to summon mystical power for duping the enemy, hunting buffalo, securing revenge, stealing horses, or making war. Contemporary Sun Dancers aspire to acquire good health for themselves and for others, safety for a loved one in the military, or power for a more positive destiny. "The importance of the Sun Dance to the Crows," Heywood avowed, "it is spiritual, for the healing, for the good luck, a good life, and for the religious."

Since William Big Day reintroduced the Shoshone Sun Dance in 1941, based on Rainbow's instructions from his Medicine Fathers, the Crows have ceased to practice the *piercing* method (as the Lakotas still do). This way featured the dancer skewering his chest, arms, or back with eagle talons (or sticks) that were fastened to a thirty-foot-long leather cord which, in turn, was tied to the Center Pole. The participant would run to and fro, leaning back and stretching the tether, enduring the pain until the flesh tore. Visions and medicine would usually accompany the excruciating torment.

Since the 1970s, the significance and popularity of the Sun Dance among the Crow people have expanded markedly. Father Randolph Graczyk, the Catholic priest from Pryor, contended, "I think there are a lot more people that dance now than did, say, fifteen or twenty years ago. At that time, as far as I can recall, there was usually one Sun Dance a summer.

Now there can be three or four!"

"In recent years there has been hardly enough room for all the dancers in the Sun Dance lodge," preeminent medicine man Tom Yellowtail explained. "It has even been necessary to make a special extension of the lodge in order to accommodate all the dancers. It is good to see so many come to participate. My heart is very, very happy to see new members, but it is not the number of people who participate that is important but their sincerity and attitudes" (Yellowtail, 181).

The Golden Anniversary had 104 dancers, an unusually large number. Because the Big Lodge is an Indian religion, Crows and those from other tribes were given priority to enter. If the whites who wanted to be involved had been admitted, then the numbers would have swelled considerably, greatly overcrowding the lodge. Phil Beaumont, Big Day's clan brother, brother-in-law and official announcer observed, "I would say there's an increase in participation especially. I mean, Heywood had to turn some people away. It was so crowded in there already. So you can see that the people really took an interest. This is work performed by the hand of God. That's the way I see it. So it's increasing. It's always increasing!"

The 1991 Sun Dance required that immense amounts of work, time, energy and money be spent by the Big Day family, relatives, and supporters in order to make Heywood's dream a reality. Years of thought, months of preparation, weeks of toil and days of individual steps in the project were invested. To the Great Spirit thousands of prayers were sent, which matched the thousands of dollars spent—money gathered by Big Day's sale of some of his own land, as well as by the contributions of those who believed in his intentions and sincerity.

Without its 104 inhabitants, the Sun Dance lodge looked like a skeleton of its former self. The cattail beds in each of the dancers' now-empty stalls verified the structure's use. The blue and white flags, which gently fluttered in the breeze, belied the tumultuous struggles, sacrifices and suffering that had transpired for three days. From the stalls to the Center Pole ran 104 individual paths where bare, dancing feet had worn away the grass. The dusty trails were like ghost shadows of the leather cords that physically attached Crow Sun Dancers to the Center Pole in the days when they pierced themselves with eagle claws and rawhide thongs. And at the base of the hub tree were hundreds, maybe thousands, of extinguished cigarettes, not only depictive of many prayers to *Akbaatatdía* but also emblematic of the deaths of the Sun Dancers' old ways.

The Golden Anniversary Big Lodge was left standing; it now had a spirit of its own. Not to be recycled for another purpose, as tepee poles may be, the Center Pole, twelve perpendicular aspens, twelve diagonal rafters and the fir trees around the periphery would remain for a long time to come as a testament, a monument to the One Divine Being, and to those who prayed to Him. "So that's why my dad told me to leave it alone," Heywood advised. "It has its own spirit which goes on and on. But once it gets down to the bottom, on the ground, my dad told me to pick it up and take it along the creek bank. Set it down and leave it there. Don't burn it or do anything with it. Just leave it there. It's not yours and it belongs to Mother Nature. So give it back to her."

The Big Lodge that William Big Day reintroduced to the Crows in 1941 continues even today. It is but another breath in the life of this vital Indian religion. For now, the ceremonial drum is silent, but the throbbing hearts still beat to the pulse.

"There is no end to these things," Heywood declared with utmost conviction. "It just goes on and on forever. It's like the water flows down to Pryor Creek and down to the river and down to the ocean. So it still continues goin' on, in our lives ... that's exactly what happens. Anything that we talked about it, from the buffalo to the trees, from the songs to the

From the stalls to the Center Pole ran 104 individual paths where bare, dancing feet had worn away the grass.

BEFORE AND AFTER HIS GOLDEN
ANNIVERSARY BIG LODGE, HEYWOOD BIG
DAY PREPARED HIS BODY, MIND AND SOUL
IN THE LITTLE SWEAT LODGE.

prayers, to the people, there's just no end to it. It keeps goin' on, around the world, around the clock, and keeps on a-goin'!"

Aho! Aho!

BIBLIOGRAPHY

Books

1. Linderman, Frank B. *Plenty Coups, Chief of the Crows*. Lincoln, NE: University of Nebraska Press, 1930.

2. Nabokov, Peter. *Two Leggings, The Making of a Crow Warrior*. Lincoln, NE: University of Nebraska Press, 1967.

3. Voget, Fred W. *The Shoshoni-Crow Sun Dance*. Norman, OK: University of Oklahoma Press, 1984.

4. Yellowtail, Thomas (as told to Michael O. Fitzgerald). *Yellowtail, Crow Medicine Man and Sun Dance Chief, An Autobiography*. Norman, OK: University of Oklahoma Press, 1991.

Interviews

1. Beaumont, Philip (Crummett, interviewer). Pryor, MT: 11/14/1992.

2. Berg, Mary Elizabeth Rondeaux (Crummett, interviewer). Billings, MT: 10/19/1992.

3. Big Day, Bill (Crummett, interviewer). Billings, MT: 11/17/1992.

4. Big Day, Heywood (Crummett, interviewer). Billings, MT: 10/5/1992 and 10/7/1992. Pryor, MT: 12/6/1992.

5. Big Day, Mary Lou (Crummett, interviewer). Pryor, MT: 11/13/1992.

6. Big Day, William (Voget, interviewer). Pryor, MT: 1946.

7. Fedullo, Mick (Crummett, interviewer). Pryor, MT: 10/20/1992.

8. Graczyk, Father Randolph (Crummett, interviewer). Pryor, MT: 10/20/ 1992 .

9. Plain Bull, Gordon (Crummett, interviewer). Pryor, MT: 11/13/1992.

10. Smells, Clara Rides Horse (Crummett, interviewer). Pryor, MT: 10/21/1992 .

THE FIFTIETH ANNIVERSARY
CROW INDIAN SUN DANCE

A Special Section of Color Photographs by Michael Crummett

BREAKING THE NEAR STILLNESS OF THE
FIRST NIGHT, A WARM ORANGE AURA OF
THE COMING DAYSTAR MELTED AWAY THE
INDIGO HEAVENS AND HAILED A HISTORIC
FIFTIETH ANNIVERSARY SUN DANCE.

At one of the preparatory
Medicine Bundle Opening
Ceremonies in Pryor,
Montana, Heywood Big Day
and Samuel Plain Feather,
in gestures and spirit akin
to those of an actual
Sun dance, prayed to
Akbaatatdía (The One
Divine Being) by blowing
on eagle bone whistles.

CARSON WALKS OVER ICE
RECEIVED HOLY TOBACCO
AND A LIGHT FROM
HEYWOOD BIG DAY, JR.,
AT ONE OF THE OUTDOOR
PRAYER CEREMONIES
BEFORE HE RECOUNTED A
PERSONAL WAR DEED IN
WHICH THE FIRST MAKER'S
INTERVENTION AND
PROTECTION SAVED
HIS LIFE.

BEFORE THE BISON HUNT,
HEYWOOD BIG DAY IMPLORED
"OLD MAN SUN" TO PROVIDE
AN INJURY-FREE, SUCCESSFUL
OUTING ATOP THE
BIG HORN MOUNTAINS.

WHEN THE FIRST SHOT WAS FIRED, A SMALL HERD OF BUFFALO MADE A BEELINE FOR SAFETY ALONGSIDE AN OLD OSTRACIZED BULL ON A DISTANT RIDGE.

THE CROW TRIBAL GAME WARDEN SLIT THE BUFFALO COW'S JUGULAR VEIN AFTER BILL BIG DAY'S SINGLE BULLET BROUGHT DOWN HER 1500-POUND BODY .

Opposite page: Heywood Big Day tied his white handkerchief around the forked lodgepole pine that would serve as the "chief" pole (number one rafter) of the Sun Dance Lodge.

Before felling the cottonwood tree that would become the spiritually significant Center Pole, Heywood Big Day offered prayers to the Almighty on wisps of holy smoke from his peace pipe.

Most of the men at the Sun Dance encampment joined together in raising the Center Pole on the exact spot where the 1941 cottonwood conduit was erected.

With the construction of the Sun Dance lodge completed, Stanley Bell Rock and John Pretty On Top brought the sacred buffalo head and bald eagle that were affixed to the Center Pole.

To the beat of drum and song, the dancers begin each day by "whistling up" the sun during the special sunrise service.

OPPOSITE PAGE: SUN DANCE CHIEF JOHN PRETTY ON TOP WHISTLED ON HIS EAGLE BONE AND SUMMONED AKBAATATDÍA (THE ONE DIVINE BEING) FOR SPIRITUAL HELP.

SUN DANCE SPONSOR-CHIEF HEYWOOD BIG DAY PRAYED TO THE ONE DIVINE BEING FOR THE PARTICIPANTS, FOR CROW PEOPLE, FOR INDIANS EVERYWHERE AND FOR ALL HUMANITY.

PREEMINENT CROW MEDICINE MAN AND SUN DANCE
CHIEF THOMAS YELLOWTAIL WAS ENGULFED IN A SEA
OF PENDLETON BLANKET COLOR AFTER THE SUNRISE
SERVICE. DANCERS GATHERED AROUND HIM AND THE
FIRE CIRCLE TO SMUDGE THEMSELVES IN CEDAR SMOKE.

A WHITE FLAG SYMBOLIZING DAYLIGHT, PURITY AND
THE EARTH—AND A BLUE FLAG REPRESENTING HEAVEN,
NIGHT AND A CLOUDLESS SKY—HUNG FROM EACH FORK
OF THE COTTONWOOD CENTER POLE.

From coals of the interior fire, several smaller fires were started outside the "Big Lodge" after the Sunrise Ceremony, so that mingling participants and supporters could cedar-smudge, bless and warm themselves over the Sun Dance embers.

TOP: DURING FOUR DAYS OF PRAYER, FASTING AND PHYSICAL SACRIFICE UNDER THE HOT SUMMER SUN, 104 PARTICIPANTS DANCED CONTINUOUSLY FROM THEIR STATIONS TO THE CENTER POLE.

SUN DANCERS STOOD AT ATTENTION DURING THE "FLAG CEREMONY" ON THE SECOND DAY WHEN VETERANS WERE REMEMBERED.

DANCERS PAUSED AT THE "SUNRISE CEREMONY" FOR INTROSPECTION AND
SELF-REALIZATION AS THE ASCENDING SOLAR ORB SWATHED THEM IN
GOLDEN LIGHT.

TO AND FRO, THE PARTICIPANTS CHARGED THE BUFFALO IN AN EFFORT TO
SECURE THE "DANCING SPIRIT" AND THEN "TAKE A FALL," WHICH ULTIMATELY
LED TO A VISION, NEWFOUND MEDICINE AND/OR POWER.

MANY MOONS AFTER THE CEREMONY'S CONCLU-
SION, THE SPIRIT OF THE GOLDEN ANNIVERSARY
SUN DANCE LIVES ON WHILE ITS REMAINS
GRADUALLY RETURN TO MOTHER EARTH.

About the Author

Author-photographer Michael Crummett was first introduced to the Crow people as a VISTA volunteer in 1971. His friendship with Heywood Big Day spans many years and he is regarded as a member of the Big Day family. Mr. Crummett's photography has been widely exhibited in museums and galleries throughout the West. His articles and photographs have appeared in such books and magazines as *Northern Lights*, *Outside*, and *Montana's Indians: Yesterday and Today*. He is currently working as northern plains field photographer and consultant to Time-Life Books on *The Buffalo People*. He lives in Billings, Montana, with his wife and two sons.

The small symbol appearing at the top center of each page in *Sun Dance* is not a design for design's sake. It is Heywood Big Day's personal Sun Dance emblem, which he received during a Big Lodge ceremony in Idaho. This sacred design adorns Mr. Big Day's Sun Dance skirt and was reproduced with his permission.